POETRY STUDIO

PROMPTS FOR POETS

TYLER MILLS

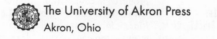
The University of Akron Press
Akron, Ohio

ISBN: 978-1-62922-285-1 (paper)
ISBN: 978-1-62922-286-8 (ePDF)
ISBN: 978-1-62922-287-5 (ePub)

A catalog record for this title is available from the Library of Congress.

The paper used in this publication meets the minimum requirements of ANSI NISO Z 39.48–1992
(Permanence of Paper). ∞

The views contained herein are those of the individual authors and do not necessarily reflect the
views of the editors, the Akron Series in Contemporary Poetics, or The University of Akron Press.

Cover: Photo from iStock.com/bombermoon. Cover design by Rhye Pirie.

Poetry Studio was designed and typeset in Garamond with Futura titles by Amy Freels.

Owing to limitations of space, permission acknowledgments begin on page 239.

Produced in conjunction with the
University of Akron Affordable Learning Initiative.
More information is available at
www.uakron.edu/affordablelearning/

For the poets who came before us, who write with us,
and who have yet to take their first breath

Akron Series in Contemporary Poetics
Mary Biddinger and John Gallaher, Editors
Nick Sturm, Associate Editor
Jordan McNeil, Associate Editor

And as imagination bodies forth
The forms of things unknown, the poet's pen
Turns them to shapes
—Shakespeare, *Midsummer Night's Dream*

Contents

Moving through Story, Movie, Myth

Welcome to the Poetry Studio

Sometimes, I'm asked, *How do you have time to write?* Or, *You must have a regular writing schedule?* To the first question, I answer, *I don't!* And to the second, also, *I don't!* In fact, I feel like I'm hardly ever writing. Or that when I'm writing, I'm doing something else at the same time: taking a break from grading, making notes for a poem while stirring a pot of pasta, mumbling a line to myself on the subway so I don't forget it before I can type it into my phone. I like to send texts to myself with poetry ideas; I often wonder if someday, I'll mistype the phone number and send some dreamlike language to an unsuspecting stranger. Last week, a random stranger texted me a photo of a bottle of champagne, so who knows!

The thing, though, that keeps me writing is to tell myself that even if it's only once a week, I can claim twenty minutes that are fully mine. I can enter a studio— an art studio, recording studio, dance studio, yoga studio, or a basketball court— in a corner of my mind and lock the door. With this time, in this mindset, I can jot down my thoughts, rethink my revisions, or return to a poem from weeks ago.

The purpose of this book is to welcome you to your own studio, a poetry studio. These prompts are meant to activate ideas and invite you into a space where you can create something even when you might not feel creative. The poetry studio is a place where you're given some materials to help you create. There is no blank page here. Language is here. Memory is here. Tangible details. Songs. Movies. Scraps of conversation. Animals. Winter walks.

The poetry studio is warm, always unlocked, and the windows are letting in a cool breeze. The floors are clean and bare—ready for what you bring with you. You are a poet. You are here. This poetry studio is a space outside of time. What I mean is that even if you only have twenty minutes, you can open a door into time and, using these prompts, find the poem you are already carrying inside of you.

Can you reuse these prompts? Yes. Will you write completely new poems? Yes! Just like you might show up to a studio wearing the same sweatshirt, noticing the same slant of light coming in through the window, bringing your body and soul, your memory and intention—all of these things will create new energy for your movements, both inner and outer, each time you find yourself engaging with one of these prompts.

I created these prompts for poets of all levels—in courses I've taught, in newsletters I've shared. And for myself. You might be in an MFA program or a college class. You might be writing your first poem. You might have retired and are finding yourself returning to writing. You might be a published poet. No matter your experience with poetry, these prompts are meditations and invitations for you to *write poems*. These are paths you can follow to your own ends. This studio is here for you, and this space will guide you into finding your creative voice so you discover the poet inside of you even on a day you think they are hiding from you.

These are not deeply formal explorations (there are already wonderful books in existence you can pair with this one if you'd like a primer on form, such as Mark Strand and Eavan Boland's *The Making of a Poem: A Norton Anthology of Poetic Forms*), though there is a "Sonnet Yourself" exercise in this book. Instead, these prompts are invitations for you to find your way into writing new poems and discovering what is at stake for you in what you want to say. You might know you want to write a love poem. But how to begin? You might know you want to write a poem about movies, but from what angle? The poetry studio is a place where you can move and express what you want to, at any time. In a café, at a beach, on a writing residency, in a classroom, in your kitchen, in your car. This book can travel with you, tucked into a backpack or handbag.

With each prompt, I've offered a poem that is in conversation in some way with how I'm inviting you to stretch and play. My question for you to think about when reading them is *What does it feel like to be in the same room as these poems?* Your voice is individual—*yours* only—and the prompts I've written invite you to activate your inner vision and ear.

When I sit down to write, I love to read poems that I feel might be in conversation with what I am thinking about—with what is tugging my sleeve and leading me to my desk. Similarly, I've offered poems that can do this for you. These are poems I love and poems that connect in some way with the prompts. If you decide, on your own, to engage closely with an element specifically from a sample poem offered here, you should add an attribution like "after X" underneath the title of your poem. But I'm not encouraging imitations; in fact, these prompts lead you *away* from the poems I've shared and into *your own* imaginative landscape.

This poetry studio is a place you can enter even when you feel like you aren't in a particularly creative mindset. And yet, there is always a way into the germ of an idea. I remind myself of this even on days when that feels impossible. I've included brief meditative steps to unlock the magic lingering just underneath the surface so that you can open up this book and begin to create something new. A poem that is truly yours.

In a world full of noise, it is special that you are a poet. If you are reading this book, it is *because* you are a poet. You are here, honoring your craft and voice. I am grateful to you for being here. What you have to say has value.

Words create real change in the world.

The studio door is always open. You are here now, yes.

But you have always been here. You are a maker. Your voice is waiting to speak.

Welcome to the *Poetry Studio*.

Before We Begin

As you read these prompts and begin your poems, try brainstorming ideas for them with a pen or pencil on paper before turning to the computer. Grab a cup of coffee or tea, a favorite snack, a notebook and pencil or pen, and you're ready to begin.

Speaking of notebooks and pens, you don't need anything fancy! I like to write in a cheap sketchbook. And sometimes, I'll write on the back of an envelope. My pen of choice is a blue Bic—it's not even comfortable to hold. But it reminds me of taking notes with a friend in science class in sixth grade. We were always on a quest to find a blue pen that matched the color of our jeans. We'd scour the floor under the desks before class to add pens to our collection and test them out in our notebooks while we learned about the solar system. All of this is to say that you already have all of the materials you need. Maybe you have a favorite pencil or a pen you picked up at a hotel or dollar store or classroom floor and some blank pages of paper from your printer. Your poems are inside of you already, and the most important part of the equation is *you*.

Let go of the inner critic that might try to interrupt you. Your ideas are good. Invite in what comes and don't self-edit while you are creating. You can prune later.

There are revision prompts located at the end of this book for when you're ready to jump back into your drafts. You're welcome to flip through the book and read them now. You're welcome to save them for when you're ready.

Now, as you enter the studio, welcome what you bring with you. The room is yours. Come as you are—today.

You are enough. You have everything you need already inside of you.

Into the World

Seasonal Encounter

This prompt is inspired by Kim Addonizio's "New Year's Day." I love how Addonizio's poem explores the landscape of winter, the sounds and textures of the speaker's walk, and how the past emerges. I, too, love the skepticism that enters the poem. What does it mean to create meaning out of the past? How do we remain rooted in the present?

Go outside and encounter the world, however you can, even by walking from your door to the road and back or looking out of the passenger seat of a car window. Notice everything you can around you, and maybe even take a notebook with you so that you can write down details: cars, trees, garbage, people, animals. Aim to notice colors.

Draft a poem where you try to transform one of the things you see into a comparison with something in your life (through a simile or metaphor). Develop this in the poem, and then question the image as you near the poem's end. Try to repeat the phrase "I don't think" more than once.

Try your poem in couplets (two-line stanzas, or groupings) or tercets (three-line stanzas, or groupings).

New Year's Day

Kim Addonizio

The rain this morning falls
on the last of the snow

and will wash it away. I can smell
the grass again, and the torn leaves

being eased down into the mud.
The few loves I've been allowed

to keep are still sleeping
on the West Coast. Here in Virginia

I walk across the fields with only
a few young cows for company.

Big-boned and shy,
they are like girls I remember

from junior high, who never
spoke, who kept their heads

lowered and their arms crossed against
their new breasts. Those girls

are nearly forty now. Like me,
they must sometimes stand

at a window late at night, looking out
on a silent backyard, at one

rusting lawn chair and the sheer walls
of other people's houses.

They must lie down some afternoons
and cry hard for whoever used

to make them happiest,
and wonder how their lives

have carried them
this far without ever once

explaining anything. I don't know
why I'm walking out here

with my coat darkening
and my boots sinking in, coming up

with a mild sucking sound
I like to hear. I don't care

where those girls are now.
Whatever they've made of it

they can have. Today I want
to resolve nothing.

I only want to walk
a little longer in the cold

blessing of the rain,
and lift my face to it.

Touching the Stones
Doorways and Floors

Lucille Clifton's poem "far memory" begins, "my knees recall the pockets / worn into the stone floor." Knees on the worn stones, hands touching brick—these tactile details launch the poem into a meditation about the memories a place can hold. In another of Clifton's poems, "memory," the speaker reveals how one person can remember a scene so differently from another—the girl who finds herself "remembering your mother's face / turned to water under the white words / of the man at the shoe store" while her mother says "it never happened." Who remembers what and why?

Memory and touch are so closely connected: the tactile can invite into the imagination the memories a place can carry. We also feel memory's touch as personal—as individual.

This prompt invites you to meditate on touch, memory, and place. How can place offer up its own memories into our imagination? How can we personalize these memories of place? In what ways might our recollection of an event differ from someone else's?

    1.   Before you write, take a moment to ask yourself these questions and jot down answers, phrases, and even individual words that come to you: What doorways do I remember? What did they look like? How did I feel passing through them? What floors do I remember? What do I remember about these floors? (Colors, textures, patterns?) Why do I think I remember them? What memories, mine or of the place itself, come to mind as I think of any of these doorways or floors?

2. Now ask yourself this: Would I remember any of these spaces/places differently than someone else in my life? What would someone in my life say happened or didn't happen here?

3. You are ready to begin your poem. Start with tactile descriptions of one of the doorways or floors that tugs at your memory the most, making sure to include at least one color. Allow the poem to fold in details from your brainstormed notes. Include what someone would say didn't happen here. Try to include two questions in your poem. If your mind meanders and builds a scene unexpectedly into your poem, let this scene in.

Aim for fifteen to forty lines, with relatively shorter lines if you can.

Tip: After you build and build your poem with detail and memory, ask yourself what (if anything) you might gently trim to let the most vivid lines sing.

memory

Lucille Clifton

ask me to tell how it feels
remembering your mother's face
turned to water under the white words
of the man at the shoe store. ask me,
though she tells it better than i do,
not because of her charm
but because it never happened
she says,
no bully salesman swaggering,
no rage, no shame, none of it
ever happened.
i only remember buying you
your first grown up shoes
she smiles. ask me
how it feels.

Outside Today, Inside History

If possible, plan a time when you can be outside*—a balcony, a patio, a porch, a garden, a park, a front stoop, etc. Bring a notebook. On this day, what do you see *and what did you need to do in order to be where you are*? Be still for a few minutes, and then jot down visual impressions like objects, colors, and movements. Listen to what is around you: What do you think you hear vs. what are you hearing? What do you expect to hear but don't? What made it possible for you to be where you are right now? Be as specific as you can in your notes. Last, make a note about something new that you learned this week—something you genuinely did not know until this week. Now, draft a poem that begins "Today, instead of _____, I _____" and begin incorporating your notes. Write a poem longer than fourteen lines. Write longer or shorter lines than you usually do. Once you've finished your draft, you might choose to keep the phrase "Today, instead of _____, I _____," or you might decide the poem can slip its shoulders out of it now and trim it!

* This exercise can be done at an open window as well.

I Ask the Garden for Comfort

Luiza Flynn-Goodlett

So she pulls me down

beside the earthworm my

shovel halved, prods until

both sides flex. A few bees

remain to crawl the lupine's

purple throats and emerge

yellow, hawks to cry from

their nest in the oak's heart.

Yes, bougainvillea is more

fuchsia than thorn, nature

brutal, not cruel—watches

us rot, be eaten alive, but

won't recognize borders,

obey laws, work an hour.

Even when long thought

dead, she'll stay secreted

in fungi until our voices

fade, and then emerge

to green over footprints.

The Everyday Sacred

What are the most special things you have in your home? (By *things* I mean nonliving!) Where do you keep these objects—or the most special one—and why? We all have trinkets like these, knickknacks given to us, specific books picked up at a used bookstore, handwritten notes from a friend or a relative, or maybe an article of clothing we don't wear anymore but can't give away. These are the things that we carry with us despite any boxes soon-to-be marched out the door to Goodwill. These objects, over time, become almost sacred, whether they are gifts from people who are no longer alive, tools we use occasionally but save for the rare times they're needed, or little things that we've kept for one reason or another over the years.

This prompt invites you to think about what *surrounds* the special thing in your home. I'm talking about the immediate context of your life that bumps up against or brushes across the special object: the items *around* the thing in the drawer, on the shelf, in the box. What lives next to the sacred object? What keeps it safe? Or what has just happened to be stored next to it?

Do any of the things *next to* the special object, by proximity to it, become special?

1. Think about the most special objects you have in your home. If it's helpful, take a brief tour of your living space and think about what you hold and where. You don't need to rummage through a closet. You can do a quick walkthrough and make a mental note about anything that springs to mind—anything that you have for some reason kept. Try to list four objects and where you keep these objects.

2. Now, think about which of these objects you can't get out of your mind right now. Maybe it's something that you now wonder why the heck you've kept it. Maybe it's something special that you haven't taken out of its storage place for a while. Maybe it's a unique kitchen tool that is kind of wonky, but you swear by it. Or maybe this object is something that without a doubt you rank as *the* special thing in your home, and you hold it, look at it, listen to it, or use it all of the time. Whatever the object is, underline or circle this particular item on your list.

3. Here's the twist! Now that you've chosen your sacred object, picture where you keep it in your living space. (Not where you intend to keep it, but where it lives right now.) Make notes about this location and use colors and textures to describe the things that touch the object or occupy space near it.

4. Begin a poem with "Not the_[sacred object]____, but __[one thing nearby]_____" and recall details about all of the items near the sacred thing. Can you describe these ordinary objects with language that render them sacred, too? Can they become special? What functions do they have? Aim to use at least two metaphors in your poem. And let your poem travel! Your poem might lead you to a memory. Make sure to jot it down even if you aren't sure how this tangent might relate. Invite what comes to you into this poem.

5. Once you've written your poem, try to organize it into couplets (two-line stanzas). Make sure that you've enjambed, or broken, at least one line in a really unexpected place. (But don't go overboard!)

Love Letter with Nightguard and Liam Neeson

Kendra DeColo

Stoic and stately bouncer of the world's smallest
strip club, I am delighted every time I pull you out

like a Sunkist can from a creek
so I can say *good morning* to my husband,

delighted my teeth survived the night
cloaked in their velvet slurry

like a monk feral beneath his robe
delighted to feel my tongue do their figure eights

on the roof of his mouth even though,
let's be honest, we are middle-aged

and married and the last time we morning-
fucked was before my uterus swelled like a prize

pumpkin, back when we could watch a matinee
directly after, still wet with 11 am, a giant cup of soda

sweating between us under the glow
of Liam Neeson, surly as a saint

or Tom Hanks cowering in his ship,
waiting for that perfect line (say it with me)—

I am the captain now—whoever thought I would miss
watching a past-their-prime star

pay off his alimony, Liam Neeson
hovering above us like a renaissance angel,

that years later I would whisper his words
into my husband's ear (say it)

"what I do have are a very particular set of skills"—
and it would almost transport us back

to when we could sit in the dark sipping
collective air—

Oh guardian of syllables, flash dancer in the supermarket aisle
of anxiety where the only things left are musky bottles of Mountain Dew—

I used to love rest stops, the constellations of key chains,
lighters with zodiac signs, and silk-screened wolves, oh the wolves—

Did I start grinding my teeth then when the world first signaled its descent,
the two halves of my body swing dancing

as if pressure might crown a spark, my mouth a parking attendant
in God's strip mall holding her citations

and spitting out a star—
Lord, I want to taste everything now that oranges are hard to come by,

want to know what my husband feels as his mouth circles the perimeter
of an ice cream sandwich, his teeth glimmering

like the shores of my childhood where treasure
proliferated from the ocean's inky jaw

steadily grinding against itself—the way
anything is ever born, Liam Neeson

struggling through a movie
so bad it becomes the only one I want to remember.

Politics at the Playground

Maybe it's because I've been spending a lot of time at playgrounds lately, but the politics that erupt there are so much more multifaceted and nuanced than I ever realized. The more I think about it, the more I can remember the ways that playground play revealed something more about myself, about my life, and about the world around me, even if I didn't understand fully what was happening at the time. And now, interactions between three- and four-year-olds, between preteens, and between adults that I glimpse when I'm at a playground make me think about the ways these spaces are constantly inscribed and reinscribed with meaning, with the politics embedded in social interactions.

The metal bars and swings that could almost take you skyward if you pumped your legs high enough—who doesn't want to fly to the sun, yes, like Icarus, this time, this last pump of the legs will get you there, right? What do you learn when you fall?

Remember a time you were at the playground—as a child or as an adult—and witnessed or were part of an unexpected interaction. You can also think about the ways that the emptiness of playground structures when not in use might hold unexpected meaning, as in Trey Moody's love poem, "The Swing Set."

The Swing Set

Trey Moody

The first thing you texted me
that Sunday morning I stared out
at thirteen inches of snow, the snow
I piled into conquerable hills

rising from the corners of the yard
forgotten, that Sunday morning
the dog warmed the silence
of my bare feet so I could see

the neighbor's maple buds
marooning the off-white sky
and regard the foolish desire, foolish
even this lonely time of year,

for color—when your name
brightened the phone's cracked screen
the first thing you texted was
I dreamed you asked me to write a poem

about a rusty swing set. Later that Sunday
morning I remembered the image
from the sad film you stopped
watching in which two characters

are driving through upstate evening
snow to the boyfriend's family farm
when the girlfriend looks into
the passing bleakness to find

in the empty expanse sprawled
before a long-abandoned homestead
the absolute redness of a gleaming
swing set. That Sunday morning

I didn't text you a description
of something that cannot be
found. I said *now you have to write it.*
Maybe you are. Like love, that

sudden rush of color out of nothing
but inertia, offered here—
I can give you this. I can give you
that. I cannot take anything away.

Moving Into, Over, Around, and Through

This prompt invites you to investigate the way that Audre Lorde's "Movement Song" enacts movement through the pitter-patter of prepositional phrases.

1. Think about times you've left one place or state of being to go to or experience another. This could be a city, a town, an apartment, a home, a lover, a friendship, or a school. Jot down two places you've left and, if this relates to you, one relationship (romantic or friendship) you've left.

2. What are some words that relate to travel in one way or another? Make and model of a car, a kind of airplane, a bicycle, a ship, a kind of shoe, etc.? Wherever this question leads you, jot down at least four words that spring to mind.

3. Go to a cooking website. Click around aimlessly for a minute on the recipes. Jot down two kinds of foods (or food words) that you've found.

4. Write a poem in shorter lines than you usually choose that focuses on leaving one place for another place or becoming lost. You can think about the joys or the fears of leaving and being lost. The mood of the poem is up to you. Choose one or two of the examples from step one to focus on in your poem and address the place or places (or person, or people) as a "you." What was the experience like? What was the feeling like? What details come up for you as you speak to what kind of movement, or action, this was? Make sure to expand upon details

of your poem with prepositional phrases that you can use as embellishments: "in the door, in the wood, in the black hole of the lock" (as an example). Try to do this in your poem at least twice. Incorporate at least one of your travel words from step two as well as your food words from step three. Let your poem take you where it travels. Think of this as freewriting where you let your mind wander and show you where it wants your poem to go.

Once your poem is drafted, you can try for slightly longer stanzas (six lines)! There is no length requirement for your movement poem. It will take shape as you write it.

Movement Song

Audre Lorde

I have studied the tight curls on the back of your neck
moving away from me
beyond anger or failure
your face in the evening schools of longing
through mornings of wish and ripen
we were always saying goodbye
in the blood in the bone over coffee
before dashing for elevators going
in opposite directions
without goodbyes.

Do not remember me as a bridge nor a roof
as the maker of legends
nor as a trap
door to that world
where black and white clericals
hang on the edge of beauty in five oclock elevators
twitching their shoulders to avoid other flesh
and now
there is someone to speak for them
moving away from me into tomorrows
morning of wish and ripen
your goodbye is a promise of lightning
in the last angels hand
unwelcome and warning
the sands have run out against us
we were rewarded by journeys
away from each other
into desire
into mornings alone
where excuse and endurance mingle

conceiving decision.
Do not remember me
as disaster
nor as the keeper of secrets
I am a fellow rider in the cattle cars
watching
you move slowly out of my bed
saying we cannot waste time
only ourselves.

Winter Animal

This prompt invites you to think about and meditate on winter animals and creatures. Jot down a list of birds, dogs, cats, snakes, coyotes, bears (or any animal!) that you have seen in a winter landscape. This landscape might be a Midwestern snowbank or a California rain shower. A New York slush puddle or a desert arroyo. Next to your list of creatures, make notes about the landscape where you saw the creature. Now, choose one animal to focus on—the one that seems the most vivid to you now. Jot down two colors, one of the animal and one of the landscape. Write down three kinds of movements that the animal made in the scene. And write down a mood—any mood.

Now, begin a poem where you try to evoke the mood you chose by describing the winter animal in the landscape where you experienced this creature. Invite its movement into the poem. Bring color in. Ask two questions in the poem: one of the creature and one of the self. Write a poem longer than fourteen lines.

Bonus: Once you have a draft of the poem, change its form. (If you had a poem in one long column, break it up into stanzas! If you had a poem in couplets, try out quatrains. You may even consider introducing unexpected gaps within the lines to allow the breath of the page into the poem.)

White Dog

Carl Phillips

First snow—I release her into it—
I know, released, she won't come back.
This is different from letting what,

already, we count as lost go. It is nothing
like that. Also, it is not like wanting to learn what
losing a thing we love feels like. Oh yes:

I love her.
Released, she seems for a moment as if
some part of me that, almost,

I wouldn't mind
understanding better, is that
not love? She seems a part of me,

and then she seems entirely like what she is:
a white dog,
less white suddenly, against the snow,

who won't come back. I know that; and, knowing it,
I release her. It's as if I release her
because I know.

Ready, Set, Go!

For this prompt, you'll write about movement and do this in a way that switches perspective. This prompt invites action and excess! And, as I like to say, if you start this prompt and end up hiking down a different trail you want to explore as you go along, that's OK!

1. First, brainstorm a list of actions (verbs) that connect with specific performative gestures. Dance, baseball, music (performing on an instrument, singing, DJing), cycling, or a particular action during a step of a recipe (rolling dough, shaking a cocktail, skinning a vegetable are options). For example, if you're thinking about dance, brainstorm an action specific to a kind of dance. Your actions do not need to be related to one another.

2. Now that you have a list of three actions, think about if you can connect any of them in any way, even though they're very different. How are any actions similar to any other? Can you connect them through a simile or metaphor in any way?

3. Jot down a mood you want to capture. Imagine you're a filmmaker and that you are choosing mood music and a kind of pacing for the action that you're writing about.

4. Write a poem that begins with one of your gestures and describe this action with as many verbs as you can. If a memory comes up for you, or a vignette, or a scene from a film (or even an imagined scene), write into this idea. While you're writing, try to compare the action to one

(or even two) of the other actions you selected through simile or metaphor. Choose your verbs with specificity in mind and pack your poem with them. Describe the action and scene through the mood you've chosen. What is the person doing the action of losing, gaining, loving, or celebrating feeling? Can the poem reveal this through the way the actions are described?

Write a poem that is at least sixteen lines long.

Bonus: Try to switch from third person to "you" or "I" at some point in the poem.

Tip: You can try titling your poem "Poem with [Main Action] and [One thing in it]" and see if this sparks other title ideas you might have!

The Sea

David Baker

      urchins spread. They want enough room
on the seabed, along the black basaltic
jet of offshore reef, sun-pied, outswept, or
down along the darker overcrowded

urchin barrens, to quiver their hundred-
plus spines and not encroach or be encroached
or preyed upon, pulled, ripped apart by the
wolf eel, the next-to-deadliest lurking

shadow in these waters. Are more black
than not, and move, when they move, "by means of
tiny, transparent, adhesive tube feet"
by the hundreds. Though they prefer to stay.

The barrens are their own creation. Such
hunger, such efficient self-replication,
they tend to nullify what other lives
would abound in other seas. Black dandelions,

they're like a small explosion in the stilled; or
like that red-bloomed scrub bush in the cactus
gardens near our house, more scarlet than red,
whose name we haven't learned, flaring at each

air-breath like hair, so soft yet erect in
the afternoon burn like underwater
shimmers of the urchins themselves, lit red.
And red your foot—within a minute of

your step and cry—we tried to heal with cool
seawater poured over; and scrubbed the four
last snapped-off spines; then sat there on the shore.
Three boats went by. A yacht. The island

ferry hauling all the day's workers home.
Then, come night, was that a liner or our
local trash scow, far out, low-lit? You can see
the phosphorescent wake five miles from space.

Community

Think about communities you've been part of (willingly or unwillingly) or are part of now: classrooms, volunteer groups, worship groups, activist groups, commuter groups, coworker groups (past or present), inhabitants of an apartment building, of a family. What are things that your community of individuals had (or have) in common? What is at stake when you are placed in a group outside of your control? What are the ethics of being in the group that you are in?

1. Jot down at least four communities you are or have been part of. Then choose the one that you keep thinking about right now, for whatever reason.

2. What are things that your community of individuals had/have in common? What were/are some differences?

3. Write a poem from the perspective of this "We" that begins "We wanted…" and incorporate both things into your poem. Try to write this poem in shorter lines than you might be used to. What is at stake can be so big it breaks your heart. It can be something private, personal. It can be a mix of both things. Let the voice of the "we" carry you where it leads you. Don't expect to know what the "we" will say. Don't expect to know what the "I" will say if it enters the poem briefly.

We Lived Happily during the War

Ilya Kaminsky

And when they bombed other people's houses, we

protested
but not enough, we opposed them but not

enough. I was
in my bed, around my bed America

was falling: invisible house by invisible house by invisible house—

I took a chair outside and watched the sun.

In the sixth month
of a disastrous reign in the house of money

in the street of money in the city of money in the country of money,
our great country of money, we (forgive us)

lived happily during the war.

I Quit!

There, that got your attention, didn't it? This prompt invites you to think about a time when you quit or were fired from a job. Maybe you left after a long, frustrating road. Maybe you quit on a whim. Maybe you gave notice because something better came along. Maybe you were fired on a day when you least expected it. Whatever the circumstances, this prompt invites you to think about what you remember from the day that you quit and what this event meant to you.

Don't be a quitter! is a saying I first remember hearing in gym class. How often does that terrible mantra roll around the brain when we stick with a situation that we know isn't working for us? Maybe you have no choice. Until you do. Or maybe you wanted to stay and had no choice other than to leave, to be let go. Maybe you were fired or laid off, with or without notice.

What is this letting go? What does it feel like? I remember vividly the day I quit one of my server jobs. I still feel the woven belt straps of my black apron leaving my fingertips when I handed it over to my manager at the hotel bar.

What is the last straw that, on top of all the other difficulties, led you to quit a job—finally?

Or if you were let go, what did you feel like that day and what did you do after? What was this process of losing like for you? And what did you do in this moment of loss?

How can the "I" of a poem use the experience of losing a job, in one way or another, to investigate not only the nature of a kind of work, but also what a self feels, wants, and desires in a world where our experiences of time are marked by the need to earn money? In Debora Kuan's "The Night after You Lose Your Job," I'm so moved by how the poem nods to our time and place all the while accruing all of the details of daily life that go on after a job is over. I love how the ending becomes an act of grace where the speaker acknowledges her "lifetime of luck / and error."

1. Think about a time you left a job, activity, or team. Did you quit? Were you fired or let go? Maybe you can come up with a few jobs that you quit. You're welcome to make a list of options, if you can, before choosing one. (Retirement can count for this prompt, if this option speaks to you!)

2. Remember everything you can about the day you left: the weather, what you heard, what you smelled, what someone said to you. Jot down notes about these things.

3. Remember everything you can about the night and next day after (if you can). If you can't remember these things, jot down what you wish you did during this time, and be as specific as possible.

4. Begin your poem with the scene of the quitting or leaving and incorporate as many details as you can. Let your mind meander. Allow color and scent to enter your poem. You're welcome to write your poem in second person, where the poem's speaker talks to the past self directly ("You walked up to the manager…"), but this is not a requirement. Allow rage, humor, and grief in as much as your poem needs them; however, at the end of your poem, aim to look beyond the self to someone else. Try to end your poem with something that empowers the speaker.

5. As you write your poem, aim for shorter lines than are your default form. You're welcome to use "Quitting / Losing ____[Job Title]___" as a working title.

The Night after You Lose Your Job

Debora Kuan

You know sleep will dart beyond your grasp. Its edges
crude and merciless. You will clutch at straws,
wandering the cold, peopled rooms of
the Internet, desperate for any fix. A
vapor of faith. An amply paid gig, perhaps,
for simply having an earnest heart or
keeping alive the children you successfully
bore. Where, you'd like to know,
on your résumé do you get to insert
their names, or the diaper rash you lovingly cured
with coconut oil, or the white lies you mustered
about the older man in the cream-colored
truck that glorious spring day, who hung his head
out the window and shouted, "Coronavirus!"
while you were chalking unicorns
and seahorses in the drive? Where
do you get to say you clawed through
their night terrors, held them through their sweaty
grunting and writhing, half-certain a demon
had possessed them, and still appeared
lucid for a 9 a.m. meeting, washed, combed, and collared,
speaking the language of offices?

At last, what catches your eye is posted large-
font and purple: a local mother in search
of baby clothes for another mother
in need. Immediately your body is charged,
athletic with purpose, gathering diapers,
clothes, sleep sacks, packing them tightly in bags.
You tie the bags with a ribbon and set them

on the porch for tomorrow. Then you stand
at the door, chest still thumping wildly, as if
you have just won the lottery—

                and so you did, didn't you?
You arrived here, at this night, in one
piece, from a lifetime of luck
and error, with something necessary to give.

Food and Feeling

Food can satisfy hunger, fulfill a craving for something textural, unlock a memory (as in one of Proust's tea-mingled petites madeleines), conjure a feeling, or do a mixture of all of these things.

This prompt invites you to describe a particular food. Through the way that you share what it looks like or even feels like, you will convey a feeling or even larger idea. And so, the poem's feeling, idea, or message will emerge through your treatment of the subject.

In other words, the kinds of words we use to describe the pears soaked lavishly in brandy, the butchered pomegranate shedding bloody seeds, the raisin-mottled cookie dough, or the crisp toast drowning in butter will lead us to *what is at stake* in the speaker's observation of this food.

Patricia Smith's "When the Burning Begins" is a terrific example of how food can convey feeling in a poem. Consider how the poem begins with instructions for making hot water cornbread that involve waiting, burning: "When you smell the burning begin, flip it." (4). Notice how the poem shifts from this action into memory, into vignettes with dialogue. What does it mean to wait, to let the bread burn? What kind of language is used by the speaker to describe this process? How have the initial instructions changed by the time the poem reaches its conclusion?

> remember that sometimes the burning
> takes such a long time,
> and in that time,
> sometimes,
>
> poems are born (74–78).

I keep thinking about how this meditation has become an elegy and also an ars poetica, a poem about poetry.

1. Let your mind meander through memories of foods that are meaningful to you. Jot down a few sentences about foods you've seen at the store recently and/or have prepared or consumed either at home or while traveling, foods that you recall from the autumn and winter, or a favorite sweet or savory food or dish. You're welcome to make a list instead of writing your ideas in full sentences. If a food that surprises you—one that you have mixed feelings about—comes to mind, jot it down.

2. Think about which food brings up the biggest feeling—for whatever reason, even if you aren't sure why!—right now. You can choose the food that feels the most vivid, the food you can almost taste. Or you can choose the food that you find off-putting, the food that perplexes you, the food you were surprised came to mind during step one.

3. Think about what emotion you're bringing to this food. It's OK if this emotion changes as your poem unfolds or even becomes more defined. Joy can transform into pleasure. Anger into rage. Distance into grief.

4. Begin your poem by describing your food using words that are as specific as possible in the color(s), texture(s), smell(s), and taste(s) that your speaker experiences. As you describe the food, convey the emotion the speaker is bringing to each description through the kinds of words that you choose. For example, if sad, would a speaker focus on the cave-like little holes left in a half-empty pomegranate? If angry, would a speaker focus on the slippery, bleeding little seeds? As your poem develops, try to ask one question about the food that your poem does not have to answer. If a memory comes up for you as you're writing, you're welcome to allow your poem to meander and build this memory into the poem.

Bonus: Aim for three-line stanzas (tercets)!

When the Burning Begins

Patricia Smith

>*for Otis Douglas Smith, my father*

The recipe for hot water cornbread is simple:
Cornmeal, hot water. Mix till sluggish,
then dollop in a sizzling skillet.
When you smell the burning begin, flip it.
When you smell the burning begin again,
dump it onto a plate. You've got to wait
for the burning and get it just right.

Before the bread cools down,
smear it with sweet salted butter
and smash it with your fingers,
crumple it up in a bowl
of collard greens or buttermilk,
forget that I'm telling you it's the first thing
I ever cooked, that my daddy was laughing
and breathing and no bullet in his head
when he taught me.

Mix it till it looks like quicksand, he'd say.
Till it moves like a slow song sounds.

We'd sit there in the kitchen, licking our fingers
and laughing at my mother,
who was probably scrubbing something with bleach,
or watching *Bonanza*,
or thinking how stupid it was to be burning
that nasty old bread in that cast iron skillet.
When I told her that I'd made my first-ever pan
of hot water cornbread, and that my daddy
had branded it glorious, she sniffed and kept
mopping the floor over and over in the same place.

So here's how you do it:

You take out a bowl, like the one
we had with blue flowers and only one crack,
you put the cornmeal in it.
Then you turn on the hot water and you let it run
while you tell the story about the boy
who kissed your cheek after school
or about how you really want to be a reporter
instead of a teacher or nurse like Mama said,
and the water keeps running while Daddy says
You will be a wonderful writer
and you will be famous someday and when
you get famous, if I wrote you a letter and
send you some money, would you write about me?

and he is laughing and breathing and no bullet
in his head. So you let the water run into this mix
till it moves like mud moves at the bottom of a river,
which is another thing Daddy said, and even though
I'd never even seen a river,
I knew exactly what he meant.
Then you turn the fire way up under the skillet,
and you pour in this mix
that moves like mud moves at the bottom of a river,
like quicksand, like slow song sounds.
That stuff pops something awful when it first hits
that blazing skillet, and sometimes Daddy and I
would dance to those angry pop sounds,
he'd let me rest my feet on top of his
while we waltzed around the kitchen
and my mother huffed and puffed
on the other side of the door. *When you are famous,*
Daddy asks me, *will you write about dancing*
in the kitchen with your father?

I say everything I write will be about you,
then you will be famous too. And we dip and swirl
and spin, but then he stops.
And sniffs the air.

The thing you have to remember
about hot water cornbread
is to wait for the burning
so you know when to flip it, and then again
so you know when it's crusty and done.
Then eat it the way we did,
with our fingers,
our feet still tingling from dancing.
But remember that sometimes the burning
takes such a long time,
and in that time,
sometimes,

poems are born.

Summer's End

Write a poem in long lines (which I think of as longer than five beats, or ten syllables) addressed to a place during the month of August, or at a point where summer is just starting to come to an end (if you are writing this poem in a region where August doesn't mark a transition into fall!). Make sure to include three actions that an individual or groups of people are taking, three kinds of wildlife (mammals, birds, or insects), and one article of clothing. Try to incorporate at least three similes. Is the end of summer a metaphor for something else? Allow your poem to let in what comes.

Bonus: Incorporate one kind of food.

Let Evening Come

Jane Kenyon

Let the light of late afternoon
shine through chinks in the barn, moving
up the bales as the sun moves down.

Let the cricket take up chafing
as a woman takes up her needles
and her yarn. Let evening come.

Let dew collect on the hoe abandoned
in long grass. Let the stars appear
and the moon disclose her silver horn.

Let the fox go back to its sandy den.
Let the wind die down. Let the shed
go black inside. Let evening come.

To the bottle in the ditch, to the scoop
in the oats, to air in the lung
let evening come.

Let it come, as it will, and don't
be afraid. God does not leave us
comfortless, so let evening come.

Garbage: An Ode

Look in your trash can. What do you see? Make a list and describe at least five items in as much detail as possible.

Choose the one that seems saddest to you in its garbage state. Write an ode where you address the item as "you" and praise it through its uselessness. Make sure you include at least three ways it failed you (or a member of your household). Tell its origin story. Tell its story of failure (perhaps the moment it failed). Imagine another life for it. Do you have a final question for it? If so, ask it.

Epitaph by His Own Hand

Timothy Donnelly

From the morning he started
    peeling his first potato

he felt like he'd been peeling
    potatoes for eternity—

all that fell about his ankles
    like clouds' inky shadows

smudged across the pastures
    of an afterlife clearly

put farther away from him
    the harder he worked for it.

Words Recalled

Are there phrases people in your life have said to you that snag your brain? A warning, a statement, a piece of odd advice, a perhaps well-intended and yet hurtful statement? An old saying from someone you love?

This prompt invites you to use one of these phrases to begin a poem. You can wrestle with it, argue with it, name it and banish it—only you know what you need and want to do with the words that you recall, words rolling around your brain and appearing unexpectedly.

1. Brainstorm a list of people who you once knew and are no longer alive. Brainstorm a list of people you see all the time. Think about phrases that people on both lists have said (or continue to say) to you. Jot down what comes to mind. You don't need to think of a phrase for each person. The goal is to think about a group of people in your life to different degrees and to consider words and phrases that have been said to you.

2. Which phrase snags you the most right now, for whatever reason? Underline it.

3. Freewrite about why this phrase snags you even now. When recently have you thought about this phrase? Jot down the scene or context. (Location, what you were doing, who you were with.)

4. Think about a part of your body that you want to send love to. Jot it down and describe it.

5. You're ready to begin your poem. Start with the phrase (quoted) that someone has said and that snags your brain. Include details about where you were recently when you thought about this phrase and consider building this into a mini scene in your poem. Allow your poem to go where it takes you, perhaps somewhere surprising, and make sure to include the part of your body that you want to send love to. As you end your poem, ask yourself this: How do I want to reckon with the words or the phrase that I've received and carried with me?

Bonus: Try your poems in longer stanzas (five or six lines, perhaps uneven groupings of lines per stanza).

Arthritis

Carol Moldaw

"Save your hands," my mother says,
seeing me untwist a jar's tight cap—

just the way she used to tell me
not to let boys *fool around*, or feel

my breasts: "keep them fresh
for marriage," as if they were a pair

of actual fruit. I scoffed
to think they could bruise, scuff,

soften, rot, wither. I look down now
at my knuckly thumbs, my index finger

permanently askew in the same classic
crook as hers, called a swan's neck,

as if snapped, it's that pronounced.
Even as I type, wondering how long

I'll be able to—each joint in my left hand
needing to be hoisted, prodded, into place,

one knuckle like a clock's dial clicking
as it's turned to open, bend or unbend.

I balk at the idea that we can overuse
ourselves, must parcel out and pace

our energies so as not to run out of any
necessary component while still alive—

the definition of "necessary" necessarily
suffering change over time.

The only certainty is uncertainty, I thought
I knew, so ignored whatever she said

about boys and sex: her version of
a story never mine. It made me laugh,

the way she made up traditions, that we
didn't kiss boys until a certain age, we

didn't fool around. What *we*? What part of me
was she? No part I could put my finger on.

How odd, then, one day, to find her
half-napping in her room, talking first

to herself and then to me, about a boy
she used to know, her friend's brother,

who she kissed, she said, just because
he wanted her to. "Now why would I do that,"

she mused, distraught anew and freshly
stung by the self-betrayal. So much

I still want to do with my hands—
type, play, cook, caress, swipe, re-trace.

Holiday Season

The holiday sweater, the annual seasonal card (yours or someone else's), the perfect latke, the sweet dates at sundown to break a fast (ṣawm), the disastrous work party (or hilarious work party), the gift that you didn't want, the fight you wished you didn't have in the kitchen, the fight you wished you *did* have in the kitchen, the cookies, the prayers, the menorah, the kinara, the Christmas tree, the advertisements, the memorable Santa, the plane or train journey from hell, the fireworks, the unexpected moment of joy. The table you shared with loved ones. Brainstorm holiday memories using the above list as a guide.

After you have about five options, choose the one that is the most vivid to you right now. (Don't overthink it!)

Now begin a poem with "I did not want" where you describe everything that comes to mind about the thing that you chose to focus on. As you are writing, try to incorporate one thing from nature, two food items, and one rhythm element (such as two short sentences in a row, alliteration, rhyme, etc.). This might be a longer poem. Let it unwind!

The Black Santa

Allison Joseph

I remember sitting on his bony lap,
fake beard slumping off his face,
his breath reeking sweetly of alcohol,
a scent I didn't yet know at five.
And I didn't know that Santa
was supposed to be fat, white, merry—
not shaky and thin like this
department store Santa who listened
as I reeled off that year's list:
a child's oven I'd burn my fingers on,
a mini record player of gaudy plastic
I'd drag from room to room
by its precarious orange handle,
an Etch-a-Sketch I'd ruin by twisting
its dials too hard—my requests
as solemn as prayer, fervid, fueled
by too many hours of television,
too many commercials filled
with noisy children elated
by the latest game or toy.
I bet none of them
ever sat on the lap of a Santa
who didn't ho-ho-ho in jolly mirth,
whose sunken red eyes peered
out from under his oversized wig
and red velveteen cap, his teeth yellow,
long fingers tinged with yellow.
I did not find it strange
to call this man Santa,
to whisper my childish whispers
into his ear, to pull on his sleeve

to let him know I really deserved
all that I'd asked for. I posed
for an instant photo with him,
a woolen cap over my crooked braids,
mittens sewn to my coat sleeves.
No one could have convinced me
this Santa couldn't slide down
any chimney, though his belly
didn't fill his suit, and his hands
trembled, just a bit, as he lifted
me from his lap. No one could
have told me that a pink-cheeked
pale-skinned Santa was the only Santa
to worship, to beg for toys and candy.
I wouldn't have believed them,
wouldn't have believed anyone
who'd tell me Santa couldn't look
like me: brown eyes, face, skin.

What the World Knows

Begin a poem from the perspective of an inanimate object that is part of a group of other entities, and begin the poem in the third person plural: "We __[verb]___." ("We played…" "We swam…" "We sang…" etc.) Include two words that incorporate science/botany diction, two colors, two kinds of food, and one emotion. You're welcome to engage with the word categories however you like! You do not need to categorize them into separate stanzas. However, I invite you to try out three-line stanzas *or* stanzas that are each a different length. If you choose to write a prose poem, try to repeat one word within it three times.

To Bear on Us Unshaded

Hadara Bar-Nadav

We bow our heads and burn. Heat scalding the back of our necks, singeing our crowns. The sun opens over us. The sun wants to burn us into the ground. Scent of soil, glittering, cloying, sick with goodbyes. We swelter, wither, prayer stuck in our parched mouths. Birds descend, *declaim their Tunes*—piercing us with bright cries. Cardinals streak the day with blood. We follow our sad shadows, swallow our tongues. We are done. We are done. We are done.

Trees

I can't help but feel the presence of trees certain times of year, especially when bare branches create seemingly new designs in the sky or crisscross blue shadows over the dirt and pavement. Trees carry light and remain when it burns away. The light enters my windows more when the branches are bare. The trees are here and also not quite altogether here.

We're going to think about trees as a way of exploring what might be here and not quite altogether here: memory. This prompt might seem simple, but at its heart, it invites you to look at the spaces between the bare branches. What emerges? What remains hidden?

1. What are your first memories of trees? Where were you? How did you touch them? What did their leaves look like to you? What memory do these trees bring up for you? Jot down details that come to mind.

2. Do you remember the kind of tree (or trees) from step one? If not, google the kinds of trees in the area where you were living at that time and try to figure out the kind that you recall.

3. What trees are in your life now? Is there a tree you pass every day outside? A tree in your yard (if you have a yard)? A tree in the park that you pass regularly? Jot down details about this tree and how you relate to it in the present time.

4. Now think about two scents that have nothing to do with trees. Jot them down.

5.   Jot down a wish you have for yourself or for another person.

6.   Jot down two objects that have nothing to do with trees.

7.   Begin your poem with your early memory of the trees (step one), and interweave it with your current experience with trees (step two). Let your mind meander and allow the memories that come to mind to enter your poem. Incorporate the scents from step four as well as the objects from step six into your poem as it unfolds. As you feel your poem coming to a close, add your wish from step five. Try to close your poem with a detail from your earliest memory of trees.

[It's only when I look at trees]

Leah Souffrant

It's only when I look at trees—
This one—finally—reaching
Above the elevated train track
Trembling outside this window,
Glowing orange leaves scratched
On electric green, reaching
From the dirty earth—that I ask what it means
To be mortal, how we are living
Towards dying.
             Sometimes your eyes glow like that,
Lashes tipped with sunlight, glimmer
Of wetness beneath.

Landscape in Two Sentences

This poem invites you to think about a landscape of ruin and meditate on what might happen to change it, even a small thing.

Think about places you've been that seem bleak—places where you were aware of the specific details that made you especially respond to this particular landscape or structure with curiosity and unease. (Crushed glass, wilted plants, etc.) Select one place, and then jot down everything you can think of about it—and make sure to include at least three colors—and then do some research and learn about something about this place. You can pursue something you might have known on a surface level or something you previously didn't know about at all.

Begin a poem with "When…" or "Why…" Write the poem in second person (addressing the you). Try to write most of the poem in one sentence and then conclude with a separate shorter sentence. This sentence can hope for something different, will a change, offer renewal—your choice, but the goal is to change the energy of the poem.

Aim for your poem to be eighteen lines or longer.

Bonus: Try to repeat a word three times in your poem.

No Ruined Stone

Shara McCallum

When the dead return
they will come to you in dream
and in waking, will be the bird
knocking, knocking against glass, seeking
a way in, will masquerade
as the wind, its voice made audible
by the tongues of leaves, greedily
lapping, as the waves' self-made fugue
is a turning and returning, the dead
will not then nor ever again
desert you, their unrest
will be the coat cloaking you,
the farther you journey
from them the more
that distance will maw in you,
time and place gulching
when the dead return to demand
accounting, wanting
and wanting and wanting
everything you have to give and nothing
will quench or unhunger them
as they take all you make as offering.
Then tell you to begin again.

Nature, Name/Elegy, Ode

Think about places you've traveled and lived. Can you remember any flowers you have seen there? (Dandelions can count!) Research three different kinds of flowers and write down any and all names they have (common and Latin names). Now think about someone who is not here anymore and write an elegy—a poem that laments the dead—for them and incorporate the common or Latin names of these flowers. Try to place the speaker in a location in this poem: allow memory to take you somewhere specific and begin by grounding the poem there. Can you make this poem a longer poem—of twenty lines or more?

Ode to a Nightingale

John Keats

My heart aches, and a drowsy numbness pains
 My sense, as though of hemlock I had drunk,
Or emptied some dull opiate to the drains
 One minute past, and Lethe-wards had sunk:
'Tis not through envy of thy happy lot,
 But being too happy in thine happiness,—
  That thou, light-winged Dryad of the trees
   In some melodious plot
 Of beechen green, and shadows numberless,
  Singest of summer in full-throated ease.

O, for a draught of vintage! that hath been
 Cool'd a long age in the deep-delved earth,
Tasting of Flora and the country green,
 Dance, and Provençal song, and sunburnt mirth!
O for a beaker full of the warm South,
 Full of the true, the blushful Hippocrene,
  With beaded bubbles winking at the brim,
   And purple-stained mouth;
 That I might drink, and leave the world unseen,
  And with thee fade away into the forest dim:

Fade far away, dissolve, and quite forget
 What thou among the leaves hast never known,
The weariness, the fever, and the fret
 Here, where men sit and hear each other groan;
Where palsy shakes a few, sad, last gray hairs,
 Where youth grows pale, and spectre-thin, and dies;
  Where but to think is to be full of sorrow
   And leaden-eyed despairs,
 Where Beauty cannot keep her lustrous eyes,
  Or new Love pine at them beyond to-morrow.

Away! away! for I will fly to thee,
      Not charioted by Bacchus and his pards,
But on the viewless wings of Poesy,
      Though the dull brain perplexes and retards:
Already with thee! tender is the night,
      And haply the Queen-Moon is on her throne,
            Cluster'd around by all her starry Fays;
                  But here there is no light,
      Save what from heaven is with the breezes blown
            Through verdurous glooms and winding mossy ways.

I cannot see what flowers are at my feet,
      Nor what soft incense hangs upon the boughs,
But, in embalmed darkness, guess each sweet
      Wherewith the seasonable month endows
The grass, the thicket, and the fruit-tree wild;
      White hawthorn, and the pastoral eglantine;
            Fast fading violets cover'd up in leaves;
                  And mid-May's eldest child,
      The coming musk-rose, full of dewy wine,
            The murmurous haunt of flies on summer eves.

Darkling I listen; and, for many a time
      I have been half in love with easeful Death,
Call'd him soft names in many a mused rhyme,
      To take into the air my quiet breath;
            Now more than ever seems it rich to die,
      To cease upon the midnight with no pain,
            While thou art pouring forth thy soul abroad
                  In such an ecstasy!
      Still wouldst thou sing, and I have ears in vain—
            To thy high requiem become a sod.

Thou wast not born for death, immortal Bird!
  No hungry generations tread thee down;
The voice I hear this passing night was heard
  In ancient days by emperor and clown:
Perhaps the self-same song that found a path
  Through the sad heart of Ruth, when, sick for home,
    She stood in tears amid the alien corn;
      The same that oft-times hath
Charm'd magic casements, opening on the foam
  Of perilous seas, in faery lands forlorn.

Forlorn! the very word is like a bell
  To toll me back from thee to my sole self!
Adieu! the fancy cannot cheat so well
  As she is fam'd to do, deceiving elf.
Adieu! adieu! thy plaintive anthem fades
  Past the near meadows, over the still stream,
    Up the hill-side; and now 'tis buried deep
      In the next valley-glades:
Was it a vision, or a waking dream?
    Fled is that music:—Do I wake or sleep?

Landmark

Think about landmarks you have visited: ruins, churches, temples, factories, museums, ballparks. Choose one, and for this landmark, look up two native birds, two native trees, and two native flowers for the area where it is located. Write a shorter poem (fourteen lines, give or take) that explores this place using the details you gathered from the point of view of a "we" or an "I."

Bonus: Try to write your poem in tercets or quatrains.

Replica of *The Thinker*

Matthew Olzmann

By the doorstep of the museum,
the Duplicate is frustrated.
Like the offspring of a rock star or senator,
no matter what he does, it's never enough.
He only wants to think dignified thoughts,
important thoughts, thoughts that will imprint
like an artist's signature on the memory of mankind.
But it's difficult, because when he thinks,
his head is filled with iron and bronze,
not neurons and God.

I too, feel like that.
You know how it works when you make a photocopy
of a photocopy? The eye fights to see the original,
which appears blurred in each new version.
Each morning, I sit at the kitchen table
the way my father must've years ago.
I've got my oatmeal and coffee,
my newspaper and blank stare.
                                        The Replica

digs his right elbow into his left thigh,
his chin into his right fist, and then he thinks
as hard as his maker will allow. He tries to envision
patterns among celestial bodies, the mysteries
of Christ, X + Y, crossword puzzles, free will.
The expression on his face:
somewhere between agony and falling asleep.

Yet he holds this pose
as if no one will notice what frauds we are,
as if some world around him is about to make sense,
some answer has almost arrived. Almost.

Unexpected Breath

This prompt invites you to think about the ways that a gap—an unexpected breath—within a line might create a shadow meaning within the images in your poem.

How does this significant breath in the line—marked visually and spatially—offer a shadow meaning both within the line and within the pattern it makes?

I'd like you to strategically introduce such a gap—the length of a tab—within a poem more than once but fewer than six times in a stanza (or, if the poem doesn't have stanzas, in the entire poem). You're creating a pattern for a shadow meaning to enter your poem this way.

1. Imagine yourself walking through your favorite park or outdoor space, either where you live now or in a place you've lived or traveled. (Jot down three places as examples to help narrow down which place you'd like to focus on.) Now that you've chosen one, think about what you see and smell.

2. Name three plants or objects in this space. Which is the most imposing plant or object? What would it say to you if it could talk?

3. Jot down three building materials or architectural details (you're welcome to do a quick Google search for terms if this is helpful).

4. Jot down a mood (sorrow, joy, lust, anger, etc.). What makes you feel this way the most right now?

5. You're ready to begin your poem. Start with what your chosen plant or object would say to you, and meditate on what being in the space

you're imagining is like at this moment. Fold the building materials or architectural details into your poem, and make sure to bring your poem to the mood you jotted down in step four. As you write, return to the thing that the plant or object has said to you and repeat it either exactly or with a variation at least twice but no more than three times. When it repeats, add a gap within the line (the space of a tab).

Bonus: Try your poem in couplets or in stanzas!

Burial at Sea

Kimberly Quiogue Andrews

(for Ray Andrews)

Fitting   the weight of bone-ash
and its petulance   refusal to scatter
forcing us   and our rattled hearts
to make sad-awkward   jokes about
a last embrace   carbon with a will

about static cling   as our pant legs
and shoes go patchy   grey
At Great Pond   my father pours
his father into a lake   puts him out
the smoke from the cabin chimney
becomes   what it is

The difference between dragonflies
and devil's darning needles   or whatever
they're called   is that one has a body
the size   of your thumb
and the other   is so small
and jewel-toned   that we tolerate it

Over the course of many years
I continue to be   terrified
of things landing on me   as I float
in the lake   This is normal I think
it is normal to not want your body
to be docked upon   unexpectedly

Non-human animals   however
do not have   the same hang-ups so
I wonder   what it was like for the bass
to gape suddenly   over duller flies
to come up   through a surface dusted
with a strange pollen   a summer snow

I do not have   the mind of a fish
my nutrients   come from mastication
To my grandfather in the lake
who feeds   the soil that cradles it
I am sorry I flinch   from the scales
flashing greenly   in the rich water

Inviting "You" In

Write a poem where toward the end, the speaker (whether "I" or "we") becomes a "you." This you can be a version of the self, the reader, or even a combination of the two. Think of a place you visited at least fifteen years ago; this can be a place from childhood or a place from the more recent past. Think about one part of that place—a kind of tree, a room, a book, an animal—that you truly miss. Begin by describing this entity with as much detail as possible. As you work on your draft, replace the speaker with "you" as the poem moves toward its ending. Though this poem does not need to be a sonnet, aim for sonnet length (fourteen lines).

Dutch Elm

Stanley Plumly

I miss the elms, their "crowns of airy dreams,"
as Virgil calls them, their towering cathedral branching
spread into a ceiling above the lonely sidewalks of Ohio
where the first elm deaths were reported in America.
I miss in particular the perspective looking down
the distances of all those Elm-named streets disappearing
into dusk, the last sun turned the stained blue of church windows.
I miss standing there, letting the welcome dark make me invisible.
I miss the birds starting to sleep, their talking in their songs becoming
silent, then their silence. I even miss not standing there.
And I miss a life of nothing but such moments, as if they'd never
happened and all you had to go on was their memory
and the feeling in the memory forgotten but brought back
again and again because you miss someone you loved forever.

Mind & Heart

World as a Drawing

I keep thinking a lot about the *way* we look at things. Why is my eye drawn to a certain branch of a pine tree covered with moss and not another? Why do I notice the certain letter in a hand-drawn chalk sign more than another? What does it mean to observe the world for how its design catches you, tugs at you?

How might a poem begin as a kind of drawing or way of representing the appearance of something and then switch into a deeper mood, a memory, or a larger question about the world? I keep thinking of Terrance Hayes's long and wonderful poem "How to Draw a Perfect Circle," which begins, "I can imitate the spheres of the model's body, her head, / Her mouth, the chin she rests at the bend of her elbow / But nothing tells me how to make the pupils spiral" (1–3).

Whether or not you like to draw or make art, this prompt invites you to imagine capturing a shape or texture of something in the world. Marianne Moore's "A Jelly-Fish" is a wonderful example of how perceiving something deeply can evoke a sketch or watercolor painting. (In this prompt, you are welcome to wrangle with what it means to draw something, including what you might enjoy about it or what might be challenging for you!)

This prompt invites you to begin by imagining that you are drawing a detail in a familiar scene. When I am brainstorming a poem, I like to handwrite the first draft. You might especially find that this is helpful for you for this prompt.

1. Jot down a few places you have been recently (the woods, your yard, the street next to yours, the supermarket) and a few places that spring to mind from your past—places you can visualize. Favorite beach? Park bench in a city you love? Library or café? Junkyard or town dump?

2. Look at your list and without questioning why, underline or star the place that tugs at you the most right now.

3. Jot down three visual details from this place that you can picture clearly in your mind's eye.

4. Imagine drawing one of these details, and write down how you would go about this. What materials would you use? (Pencil, chalk, pen?) Which particular details would you try to illustrate and why? How? How would this be easy or challenging? Jot down your answers to these questions.

5. Begin your poem with the detail(s) from step four and allow your mind to move freely to where it will take you. Memories might enter the poem that you don't expect—let them in!

Bonus: When you have a draft, try your poem in tercets (three-line stanzas) or as one long stanza.

A Jelly-Fish

Marianne Moore

Visible, invisible,
A fluctuating charm,
An amber-colored amethyst
Inhabits it; your arm
Approaches, and
It opens and
It closes;
You have meant
To catch it,
And it shrivels;
You abandon
Your intent—
It opens, and it
Closes and you
Reach for it—
The blue
Surrounding it
Grows cloudy, and
It floats away
From you.

Mood Shift

I love Ada Limón's "Late Summer after a Panic Attack" for so many reasons, one of which is how it conveys a shift in mood through the speaker's observations of her world around her—her home, her neighborhood. What she expects to see and hear. And what surprises her: "stones / from the sea next to stones from the river, / unanswered messages like ghosts in the throat" (10–12). In this prompt, I'm inviting you to explore a shift in mood, whether from anxiety to peace, or passion to calm, or fury to acceptance, or grief to gratitude. Do this through *what* you choose to describe and *how* you choose to describe it.

1. Think about times when you've felt extreme anxiety, passion, fury, or grief. Where were you in these instances? Allow details of place to come to mind.

2. Which place is the most vivid to you right now? Which mood? Jot down the mood and the place.

3. As you recall the place, think about what *shapes* you can remember (bed, plants, window, objects, etc.). List two objects and the shape that they are.

4. Keep thinking about this place where you felt the emotion so keenly. What else comes to mind? Think of something quite usual, something you might expect to find here. Jot it down. Now try to describe it in an unusual way, perhaps using simile or metaphor.

5. Is there anything *unusual* about this place? Any objects or details that are unexpected? If so, jot this down, and describe this unusual thing with crisp details. Make it feel real and expected. Does it have a color? Note it.

6. Now you are ready to begin your poem. Begin your poem while holding in your mind the mood you've chosen and the place that corresponds with it. Describe the place and how you feel through what the speaker sees, hears, and touches. You can name the feeling in the title or the first line. But let your descriptions carry the weight of the feeling afterward.

7. As you write, try to include a question that you might ask yourself: perhaps a "How" or a "Why" question.

8. As you continue your poem, keep describing the place through the lens of the mood. How does the mood inform what the speaker notices about what's around them? Include the usual thing described so it is not ordinary and the unusual thing described to show how real and tangible it is—how it belongs.

9. After you've described the usual and unusual things, try shifting your poem to an opposite feeling by describing what is around the speaker through the lens of the new feeling. There can be a residue of the old feeling in these lines, but let the new mood in.

Bonus: What if you ended your poem with a question?

Late Summer after a Panic Attack

Ada Limón

I can't undress from the pressure of leaves,
the lobed edges leaning toward the window
like an unwanted male gaze on the backside,
(they wish to bless and bless and hush).
What if I want to go devil instead? Bow
down to the madness that makes me. Drone
of the neighbor's mowing, a red mailbox flag
erected, a dog bark from three houses over,
and this is what a day is. Beetle on the wainscoting,
dead branch breaking but not breaking, stones
from the sea next to stones from the river,
unanswered messages like ghosts in the throat,
a siren whining high toward town repeating
that the emergency is not here, repeating
that this loud silence is only where you live.

Emptying Out, Letting Go, Filling Up

Were you like me this morning and thought, *Why is my alarm going off?* Here we are, leaping into another new day! This prompt was inspired by March 15th—the ides of March—which was not only the assassination day of Julius Caesar, but also the day the Romans settled debts. What a day of weird energy, where time is a little off, more sun is etching our windows, and we move into the light marked by our relationship to the past.

I want to think more about this—settling our accounts with the past. How might a poem invite us to let go, to empty out what isn't serving us any longer, to do whatever math we have to so we can release a negative connection to something that might be pulling us down? Poems can be wishes, dreams, prayers, and even willful magic rites. Your poem can be a mixture of all of these things.

This prompt invites you to tangle with some things that you might want to let go of and imagine what you might do with these objects—or places, or even people—in order to empty out, to sing, to become ready for what might be new. The prompt also invites you to think about what can be filled up once you've let go of something. How can life can bring you something beautiful from this place of newness?

1. Think about your living space. What are some things in it that you can see or that you know are hidden in your closet or a drawer that you would like to let go of (but haven't been able to)? Jot down these things and details about them. If you need to look inside a closet or drawer, you can do that to help jog your memory!

2. Think about events in your past that you wish you could rewrite. What tugs at you the most right now? (Big or small?) Jot down details about this event (or these events). What would you do differently?

3. What are you the most grateful for in your life right now?

4. Jot down four things that are blue.

5. What is your favorite number? Don't overthink this! This can be your favorite number today. Jot it down.

6. Imagine letting go of one of the objects from step one. What would you do (real or imagined) to let go of it?

7. Begin your poem by describing one of the objects from step one and what the speaker does to let go of it. Bring the color blue into your poem through the blue things you brainstormed. Bring your favorite number into your poem. As you write, shift into the event that tugs at you: what does the speaker do to rewrite it, to let go of it? What are you grateful for? In your poem, try to use the word "we" at least once.

Bonus: Once you have a draft, try your poem in quatrains (four-line stanzas) or longer stanzas.

Filling Spice Jars as Your Wife

Kai Coggin

It seems like all my poems
after this will be different,
they will hold a different weight
like how the weight of my heart
has shifted into indistinguishable float,
into lifting cloud,
into weightless flight tonight
as the rain gently falls
on the summer-heated tin roof,
the din of casual raindrops
and warm low lights glowing
and wind blowing through the house,
we have all our doors and windows open.

We have all our doors and windows open
and I am pouring spices into glass jars,
coriander cinnamon cumin ground sage
and it's hard to describe this
moment in the confines of a page,
tiny hills of vibrant color
and intoxicating fragrance
and you hear the cadence
of my heart
from the kitchen
where you build the perfect fitting slip-in shelves
for our spices over the stove,
match the colors,
match my colors to yours,
I have all my doors and windows open to you.

I have all my doors and windows open to you
and you have come all the way inside,
sat down at the table of my deepest desires
and lit a fire to warm us both,
the wind blowing through the house,
the rain gently giving way
to turmeric sunrise
and you, darling,

you are my wife.

You are my wife
and it's like I have been waiting
my whole life
to say those words,
and I feel held in a way
I have never felt before,
to look down at my fingers
dusted with ginger and thyme
and see the gold of my wedding band
glint and shine in the warm low light glow,
I am yours
and you are mine,
promised on Zoom in our garden
of giant zinnia and hummingbird vines,
sung out in the morning song of bluebirds,
this union that ripples love out to the world
and infinities back into us again
love—
in the fine powder of these spices,
ground up essence of oregano and basil,
I see our love in every atom suddenly
and every cell in me finally exhales,
and perhaps that is the wind.

Perhaps that is the wind
blowing through the house,
this release of eternal searching
and finding you there,
calling me your forever,
naming me your always,
to have and to hold,
till death do we part and start all over again
looking only for each other's hearts,
taking my life in your hands eternal,
marrying me to the heavens,
latching me to the star-trail of your white dress,
in this orbital dance,
this lift and spin,
this knowing from within
that all my poems after this will be different

because you are my wife.

Love Poem for the World

Go to the most recent issue of the *New Yorker, New York Times, National Geographic,* or another periodical you can access. Browse headlines and excerpts, and jot down *three words or phrases* you think would be challenging to put in a poem. You might come across a headline that bothers you, a subject that you are upset by. You might come across a headline or excerpt of a story that surprises you. Perhaps you've learned something new today.

Now, think about someone or something that you would like to be the recipient of a love poem. You can think of a love poem as being romantic or as sharing the love we have for one another as humans. Address a love poem to the recipient you've chosen where you incorporate the words or phrases you've found. You're welcome to try to find a way to fold the hurts of the world into your love poem. What can the act of finding love do for a difficult subject? Try to write your poem in couplets. Is your love poem an ode (poem of praise)? If so, you're welcome to incorporate the word "ode" into your title.

Ode To the Soccer Ball Sailing over a Barbed-Wire Fence

Martín Espada

> *Tornillo . . . has become the symbol of what may be the largest U.S. mass detention of children not charged with crimes since the World War II internment of Japanese Americans.*
> —Robert Moore, Texas Monthly

Praise *Tornillo:* word for *screw* in Spanish, word for *jailer* in English,
word for three thousand adolescent migrants incarcerated in camp.

Praise the three-thousand soccer balls gift-wrapped at Christmas,
as if raindrops in the desert inflated and bounced through the door.

Praise the soccer games rotating with a whistle every twenty minutes,
so three thousand adolescent migrants could take turns kicking a ball.

Praise the boys and girls who walked a thousand miles, blood caked
in their toes, yelling in Spanish and a dozen Mayan tongues on the field.

Praise the first teenager, brain ablaze like chili pepper Christmas lights,
to kick a soccer ball high over the chain-link and barbed-wire fence.

Praise the first teenager to scrawl a name and number on the face
of the ball, then boot it all the way to the dirt road on the other side.

Praise the smirk of teenagers at the jailers scooping up fugitive
soccer balls, jabbering about the ingratitude of teenagers at Christmas.

Praise the soccer ball sailing over the barbed-wire fence, white
and black like the moon, yellow like the sun, blue like the world.

Praise the soccer ball flying to the moon, flying to the sun, flying to other
worlds, flying to Antigua Guatemala, where Starbucks buys coffee beans.

Praise the soccer ball bounding off the lawn at the White House,
thudding on the president's head as he waves to absolutely no one.

Praise the piñata of the president's head, jellybeans pouring from his ears,
enough to feed three thousand adolescents incarcerated at Tornillo.

Praise *Tornillo:* word in Spanish for adolescent migrant internment camp,
abandoned by jailers in the desert, liberated by a blizzard of soccer balls.

Conversation as Metaphor

Conversations can open up so much in a poem and invite you to try out a metaphor that can live fully in the words that two characters (or perhaps even three) say to one another.

1. Sit down and give yourself some time to reflect on recent conversations with family members or old friends that have stuck with you for one reason or another. Have you spoken with anyone about anything surprising, anything that revealed something unexpected about the past? If you're not sure how to begin, first jot down a list of the names of people you talk to regularly (Zoom, phone, in-person, or some combination). Then look at the list and brainstorm a few conversations that came up recently.

2. Choose the conversation that catches your attention and that revealed the thing that surprised you the most, either about yourself, the other person, or something about the past.

3. Write out the conversation in prose, though try to be succinct.

4. Now, look at your prose notes for the conversation and trim it down into its essential and core parts. Begin your poem with something the other person said, and try to make your lines short. Think about enjambments that cut across the sentences at times in surprising ways. As you write your poem, make sure one person in the conversation asks the other at least one question (which does not have to be answered in the poem). As you reach the end of your poem, think

about revealing the surprising piece of information as directly and also as sharply as possible. What does the other person say in response to the information they learned in the conversation?

Tip: After you have a draft, pare it down even more, even by a few words here or there.

Second Wind

Louise Glück

I think this is my second wind,
my sister said. Very
like the first, but that
ended, I remember. Oh
what a wind that was, so powerful
the leaves fell off the trees.
I don't think so,
I said. Well, they were
on the ground, my sister said. Remember
running around the park in Cedarhurst,
jumping on the piles, destroying them?
You never jumped, my mother said.
You were good girls; you stayed where I put you.
Not in our heads,
my sister said. I put
my arms around her. What
a brave sister you are,
I said.

Prayer or Not a Prayer

Jot down a list of emotions that are *not* happiness or hope; in other words, list emotions that you don't think of when you think of the word "prayer." Then choose one, and write down the first three things that come to mind right now. Then jot down two things that are in your kitchen right now that you don't expect to be there. Then think of a kind of bird you know a little bit about without looking up any information, and jot down those details. Now, write a poem in a single stanza (or strophe) that begins in the emotion that you found and can incorporate the notes you made *and* wrestles with the idea of prayer. (Your prayer can be secular; you can open up what you think a prayer is and does and challenge that in this poem, if you'd like to.) Your poem might end up being like a prayer, or it might not at all.

Google

Leila Chatti

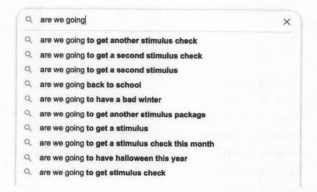

are we going	to get another stimulus check
are we going	to get a second stimulus
are we going	back to school
are we going	to have Halloween this year
are we going	to have a bad winter
are we going	to get a stimulus check this month

but where	is Chuck Norris
but where	
but where	were they going without ever knowing the way
but where	are you really from
but where	in Spanish
but where	are you
but where	's your heart
but where	's the lie

could you	be loved
could you	not
could you	repeat that
could you	please

does it	snow in Australia
does it	snow in Texas
does it	snow in North Carolina
does it	snow in Tennessee
does it	snow in Seattle
does it	snow in California
does it	rain diamonds on Saturn
does it	snow in Japan

everyone is	here
everyone is	doing great
everyone is	John
everyone is	or everyone are
everyone is	now dumber

freaked out about	COVID
freaked out about	being pregnant
freaked out about	feeling baby move
freaked out about	giving birth
freaked out about	having a baby
freaked out about	SIDS
freaked out about	dying
freaked out about	being alive

God what   should I do
God what   do you want from me
God what   is wrong with me
God what   am I doing wrong
God what   are you doing
God what   is going on
God what   did I do to deserve this

how to protect   hydrangea from deer
how to protect   chickens from hawks
how to protect   mums from frost

if I could   turn back time
if I could   save time in a bottle
if I could   write you a song
if I could   fall into the sky
if I could   then I would

joke about   2020
joke about   God sending help

keep calm and   carry on
keep calm and   carrion
keep calm and   mask on
keep calm and   wash your hands

love is   patient love is kind
love is   blind season 2
love is   war
love is   an open door

maybe this is   as good as it gets
maybe this is   how it starts
maybe this is   how it ends
maybe this is   who we are
maybe this is   the coldest winter

no I will not   have a nice day
no I will not   in Spanish
no I will not   in German
no I will not   fix your computer
no I will not   read your script
no I will not   make out with you
no I will not   elaborate
no I will not

ordinary things   cut in half
ordinary things   under a microscope
ordinary things   in an extraordinary way

please I   need help
please I   need healthcare
please I   just want to die

quiet I   can feel it
quiet I   bear within me
quiet I   can't hear the eggs

recently I   have been sleeping a lot
recently I   have been peeing a lot
recently I   sweat a lot
recently I   haven't been hungry
recently I   or I recently
recently I   was

sometimes I   don't want to be happy
sometimes I   give myself the creeps
sometimes I   run sometimes I hide
sometimes I   cry
sometimes I   feel like a motherless child
sometimes I   just want to be lonely

the truth is   out there
the truth is   like a lion
the truth is   a cave in the black mountains
the truth is   the game was rigged from the start

useless   facts
useless   information

very close   to home
very close   by
very close   to my heart
very close   veins

worrying is   a sin
worrying is   a waste of time
worrying is   like walking around with an umbrella
worrying is   like paying a debt
worrying is   suffering twice
worrying is   like praying

exactly what i   s fracking
exactly what i   s Facebook
exactly what i   s socialism
exactly what i   s COVID-19
exactly what i   s time
exactly what I   was looking for
exactly what i   t says on the tin

you could   be mine
you could   a had a bad witch
you could   say what you like
you could   in Spanish
you could   make a religion out of this

zero like   s on Tinder
zero like   s on Hinge
zero like   s on Instagram
zero like   the wind

Loving That Thing You Loathe

I recently had an encounter with a cockroach—and I *hate* cockroaches—that reminded me of other encounters with cockroaches I've had in my life, and soon I found myself sitting at my desk thinking about how much I loathe those little critters. In my mind, I listed all of the things I can't stand about those beetles. All the times they surprised me in cupboards and drains. In basement laundry rooms. And once, under a hotel pillow (I know—it was *so* disgusting). You might already know this, but in NYC, they are the size of mice sometimes. Their antennae are huge.

(I love NYC and mean no disparagement of the city itself! But the cockroaches...bleh.)

Why am I telling you this?

This prompt invites you to love something about a thing you hate.

Why?

There's a passion behind disgust that I think can be interesting to harness in a poem. What can this disgust teach you about yourself? About the world? How might this exercise stretch the imagination a bit—maybe even invite some acrobatic maneuvering, poetically speaking. (In my case, what might it mean to stop standing on a chair, step back down onto the floor, and look closely at the horrid bugs?)

I can't help but think of Aldhelm's Latin riddle, "Enigma 75" (translated by Peter Buchanan); in this case, the loathed thing speaks as the "I" of the poem. How does the poem inhabit praise through its speaking voice and the imagery the voice constructs?

1. Think about things you hate—but try to be as concrete as you can. *Things* not abstractions. Jot down a list of at least seven things. More

might come to mind the longer your list gets. Don't second-guess yourself. Nothing is too big or too small. (A kind of car! A kind of bug! An item of clothing! A brand of shoe! A kind of plant! A kitchen utensil! A medical treatment! A grooming instrument!)

2. Read your list to yourself and remember moments where you've had frustrating, infuriating, gross, or otherwise unpleasant encounters with the items on your list. The more visceral the better! After you've thought about this for a minute or two, choose the thing that leaps to mind for you in a vivid way.

3. Jot down three scenarios you can think about regarding the thing you chose.

4. Jot down four specific descriptions of the thing you chose: color, material, texture, how it moves, what it sounds like, where it lives (or exists).

5. Now, begin your poem with one of the scenarios. You can either address the thing you hate as "you" *or* you can speak in its voice, crafting a persona for it. Get as visceral and furious, disgusted, or otherwise passionate about the thing in your poem as you can through the words you choose. Include the descriptions from your brainstorm. If you can, include another scenario (or even two). As you develop the poem, think about what it is about this thing that you hate the most and why. Try to include the *why* in your poem and find one small thing to admire—even love—about it.

Enigma 75

Aldhelm, translated by Peter Buchanan

Now I row the air with paired wings
And, setting hairs on end, utter full-throated buzzes;
I dwell in a hollow trunk in thick throngs
Mixing sweet sustenance for our troops,
And yet those foods horrify human mouths.
But if someone, quashing peaceful pacts,
Desires to defile our oaken-roofed home,
I quickly call cohorts to battle,
And as we croon in crowds and thrust our spikes,
The terror-struck troops flee our flurry of darts:
So the unjustly attacked whirl our weapons,
Tips poison tinged, on our attackers.

Hornet

The Waiting Earth

Think about places you've been recently—places where you were aware of the ground. (Snow-crusted grass outside a specific house you've visited or lived in, cobblestone streets, parking lot tar, mud, sand, a tropical beach, etc.) Were you with anyone in these places? Include them. Select one place, and then jot down everything you know about the ground in that spot—what it's made of, the shapes and colors you see—and then do some research and learn about the insects, the growth, the kinds of rocks, the way the earth exists in layers, and the animals that burrow underneath your feet.

Now write down a mood—any mood.

Begin a poem where you evoke a mood by describing a specific detail of the earth in the spot you've chosen. Be as specific as you can. Then begin incorporating the details that you had brainstormed and try to write about the mood you had chosen without using any words for that mood in your poem.

Let your poem carry you into memory, into history. If you meander, by the time you close the poem, try to bring us back to the earth, to the soil, the sand, the rock, the plant.

Write a poem longer than fourteen lines.

The Whole World Is the Best Place I Ever Lived

Lynn Melnick

It's not that I don't remember
the pain of childbirth, it's that
maybe I needed it. Lately

women are brave for saying
they hate being a mother
but I've gambled on all the pain

I will bring my babies
because I have loved nothing
more than mothering. When

finally we were alone, I saw
you study me from your plastic
bassinet and I knew you knew

my ambition. I was ashamed
by all the ways I will fail you and
then flown by your forgiveness.

When you were six, mornings
you'd look for one unbroken
leaf on our walk to school to hide it

so later we could find it again
walking home. That kind of faith.
Green then red then brown then

green again, proof of longing
and immutability. Often I was
impatient. Often we were hurried

or my mind was on an irrelevant
elsewhere. But you trusted me
to come back to you and be there.

Be. There. Each afternoon
we dug through the shallow leaf
graves, your fingers my fingers

but slowly distinct. I am sorry
I will have to be finite on your
wondrous and steadfast earth.

Animating Want

What does it mean to animate the feeling of *wanting:* desire, possession, or ownership? This prompt invites you to do this from the perspective of a thing with a troubled or multilayered past (as in Rick Barot's "Galleons 1," which animates the wants of *galleons*, mercantile or war ships from the 16–18 c).

1. Brainstorm ideas for things, both large and small (a theatre or kind of theatre, a railroad track, a kind of doll, a kind of non-BPA-free plastic container...really anything). Let your mind wander.

2. Choose one object that speaks to you now, for whatever reason. Now, think about want. *Wanting.* What would this object want? Jot down whatever comes to mind, and let your mind wander. If these wants get strange, let them! These wants can be contemporary or historical (or a bit of both).

3. Write a poem that states the many things that the object you have chosen wants and try to explain some of these wants in terms of what it might feel. (You are animating an object through its desires.) How might these desires help us understand what the object is or was? Use the phrase "and then" twice in your poem.

Bonus: Try your poem in couplets!

The Galleons 1

Rick Barot

Her story is a part of something larger, it is a part
of history. No, her story is an illumination

of history, the matchstick lit in the black seam of time.
Or, no, her story is separate

from the whole, as distinct as each person is distinct
from the stream of people that led

to the one and leads past the one. Or, her story
is surrounded by history, the ambient spaciousness

of which she is the momentary foreground.
Maybe history is a net through which

just about everything passes, and the pieces of her
story are particles caught in the interstices.

Or, her story is a contradiction, something ordinary
that has no part in history at all, if history is

about what is included, what is made important.
History is the galleon in the middle

of the Pacific Ocean, in the middle of the sixteenth
century, swaying like a drunk who will take

six months to finally reach his house.
She is on another ship, centuries later, on a journey

eastward that will take weeks across the same ocean.
The war is over, though her husband

is still in his officer's uniform, small but confident
among the tall white officers. Her hair

is marcelled like a movie star's waves,
though she has been too sick with the water's motion

to know that anyone sees her. Her daughter is two,
the blur of need at the center of each day's

incessant rocking. Here is a ship, an ocean.
Here is a figure, her story a few words in the blue void.

Looking for That Place

Think of places where you traveled in childhood or during your teenage years. A grandparent's house. A hotel somewhere unusual, or perhaps not. A campsite. A cabin. A city. A cemetery. A friend's house. A train out of the city. A farm. Recall details—try to think about something unusual for each place. Freewrite a paragraph about anything that comes to mind during this brainstorm.

Next, make a list in your notebook of the three places from your freewrite that at the time were the most exciting, unusual, or even odd to you. Write down one detail from each place. (If more details come to mind right now, that is OK, and you can jot them down!)

Now, look at your list of three places. Put a star next to the one that—for whatever reason!—unsettles you the most now. This is the location that you will write about.

Begin your poem with the name of the place and the detail that struck you the most. Write a poem in first person ("I") where you imagine going back to this place and doing something you wish you did at the time. Aim for a poem longer than eighteen lines.

Abandoned House, 2002

Aaron Rudolph

I.
Summertime. The apple tree is heavy
and last year's firewood pile loiters
by the front door. Wind pushes
against the sturdy iron gate,
replaced last winter.

The apples, once yellow
and green, are now browning
with worms, the seeds of several
oozed into dirt. Years ago
apple pies escaped as air
out the windows.

Windows hang, weighted with crossing
planks. Windswept yards share a clear view
of the gutted truck in the center, its hood
standing straight like a sick tongue
stuck out, waiting for a thermometer.
The house fades from the street's landscape,
a criminal tip-toeing away.

II.
As children we lined the yard,
stray cats scattered in every corner
waiting for the moment to attack, all our weight
balanced on our toes, ready to spring
toward the tree and all the edible apples
we could hold. We ran
toward the alley, screaming—half-scared,
half-excited, our loot now in front
of us like doubloons. Mrs. Cortez
in her yard would be lobbing rotten apples
toward the street, not sure where we'd gone.
Each apple would thud the ground and break
in so many pieces, brown guts blanketing
the streets like a sci-fi movie scene
where there are aliens landing in our streets
and so many things are exploding.

Wound

Metaphor can be so powerful because it carries a story within it: the story of one thing becoming another thing. We're going to explore feeling and memory together through metaphor in this poem. We're going to think about wounds we carry with us and how describing them through metaphor can express how we feel about them.

Vievee Francis's poem "Taking It" explores relationships through the metaphor of boxing: "In love, body after body / fell beneath my own, though my own was broken" (38–39). The poem builds up to this metaphor through mini scenes of conflict, of a fight, of hurt: "I remember the falls, myself falling / to the floor or sidewalk, or against the brick wall / my head met after a push" (5–7).

As you write your poem, you can think about offering brief examples—even mini scenes—that set up the larger metaphor you're working with. Or, you can offer many metaphors where you describe the hurt using imagistic language. You're welcome to let yourself go where this poem takes you.

1. Before you write, jot down what the word *wound* means to you. What descriptions come to mind? What wounds? What might this word mean to you and why? When have you experienced a wound? What happened?

2. Jot down two foods, two kinds of buildings (places or architectural styles), and one animal.

3. Jot down three colors.

4. You're ready to begin your poem. Write about a wound, or wounds. Fold your brainstormed details into your poem. Try to describe the colors you've chosen through similes or metaphors. Try to include the foods, buildings, and an animal into the poem about the wound: you're welcome to include these items as similes or metaphors for a feeling about the wound or the wound itself. Or these items can build into a description of something that is happening in your poem. You may decide that your poem is conveying one larger metaphor, or it might include many separate metaphors. This is your story, and only you can sing its song.

Aim for ten to twenty lines. As you search for a title, try to connect it with a detail in the middle or three quarters of the way into your poem.

Taking It

Vievee Francis

for Gabby & Jen

I never remember the knuckles, though
his hand was bare, though their hands were bare.
I remember the impressions left on *this* skin, the
wilting and the welting. I don't remember the sound,
not one smack. I remember the falls, myself falling
to the floor or sidewalk, or against the brick wall
my head met after a push. There were many pushes.
Girls pushed but I punched. Pulled one
down by the hair and kneed her as my head bled.
Girls didn't punch until high school. I had always
punched. *What kind of girl are you?*
The kind who wants to live, I said, and I did want to
until I didn't anymore. But I wanted the leaving
to be on my terms, so I hit my father back.
He owned me like any good, country father, he
waited for a husband to tame what he couldn't corral,
to throw a rope like fingers 'round a neck.
When I missed a boy, fingerholds—I remember those,
and me making a fist wrongly, and punching
and I didn't mean to miss but to hit the line below the belly,
the beltline. W—— broke me in the snow
my first year North. I'm still afraid to say his name.
I wore shoes too thin for the weather (who had ever seen
such snow?) and had a Georgia lilt, like molasses
on a sore throat, sugared, raw, and he hated the sound of it.
He was black and I was black and I was so happy
to be in Detroit, and he aimed for my heart-
shaped mouth, my gapped teeth, my too-sweet tongue.
I felt the juvenile weight of him above me like snow after dark
falling steady and hard. *I'm gone teach you to talk reg'lar,*

and I stopped speaking at all. I kept my swollen mouth shut,
and a straight razor in my math book, and dreamt of a bat
cracking against his chest. A woman like me
with soft hands, not hands of the field, but
hands meant to stroke and soothe, needs a weapon,
so I studied *The Art of War* and watched boxing, and
where else was all this rage to go? Is this too dramatic?
Find another story. Find a lie. In love, body after body
fell beneath my own, though my own was broken,
and I made love like a sea creature, fluid as if boneless,
though my bones would rattle if not for the fat I cherish.
Wouldn't you? How I grew to love the heavyweights,
myself with one in the ring. How I imagined him punching
me, and punching me again, saying *I'm sorry, so sorry,
to have to love you this way.*

Delaying the Heat

This is a prompt about poem endings that invites you to delay the heat of the poem's motivating force until the very end. In other words, you'll save the thing that made you write the poem in the first place—that driving feeling and its corresponding scene, image, or action—until the final lines. I'm drawing this prompt from my poem "Occasion," which ends, "Yesterday, a boy tried / to take a stick from my daughter's hand. I wouldn't let him." These are the lines that kicked off the rumination. And I kept asking, well, why am I so furious? So instead, I created a poem that went with the fury of the *why* and then finished with the action that made me write the poem in the first place.

When I say "heat of the emotion," I'm thinking about the details, actions, or mini scenes that convey pain, horror, rage, or grief. (You can include joy here, too!) As you'll see, I did include one of my own poems here. The reason is that a student asked me how I wrote "Occasion" after they read it in *Poetry,* and I thought, *Oh, this could be an interesting exercise.*

1. Think about times you've felt something deeply (Enraged? Scared? Horrified? Sad?). No scene or memory is too small. Big feelings can come from tiny moments. In other words, you don't need to choose reading about global climate change and feeling existential dread. I'm instead asking you to think about a time when someone did something to you personally, or you had to take action to protect someone or something. Come up with a few memories and think about how they're connected to an emotion like pain, joy, horror, rage, or grief. Jot them down.

2. Choose one memory to focus on. In the clearest two to three sentences that you can, try to write down or capture the scene of this emotion (what happened / what you did). Write this in crisp language that tells us the feeling so the speaker doesn't have to.

3. Save the sentences you just wrote for the end of your poem!

4. Now, brainstorm five corresponding colors, texts, places, or foods for this feeling. Is it like driving a Prius through a snowstorm? Is it like the appearance of the ghost in Hamlet? Like a bag of half-eaten Fritos?

Begin listing corresponding images, mini scenes, or things like these that can be vehicles for the emotion in your poem. If it's helpful, you can imagine the word "Because" in front of these listed images/mini scenes. As you write, let yourself meander. Write down as many corresponding images as you can so that you end up with thirty lines for your poem. Carry the momentum as far as you can, and be as wild as you can.

5. Once you've reached the most heated listed item, the final one, then add the final lines that you saved in step three.

6. Tweak your poem a little bit so that your line lengths are five to seven beats long (if you can). The reason is that the lines shouldn't be exceptionally short or exceptionally long.

Occasion

Tyler Mills

Gatsby is not drinking a gin rickey.
Dracula not puncturing a vein.
Jack the Ripper does not knife a teenage girl
deep into her abdomen and then snake her intestines
through the town square. The birds remain in the pines.
Hunter S. Thompson isn't dropping acid in Vegas
and grabbing a woman who came to clean his room
with fresh sponges and bleach.
The room does not hold a frat boy
opening my legs. It does not cool
the man who gave me wine and refused
to let me eat and followed me to my car.
It does not have my bed after, only me
in it. I had pulled the door out of his hands,
locked the car, driven away.
The poem does not include the teenage boy
who unfurled his tongue between his pointer and middle finger,
following me on a bike while I pushed her stroller.
This isn't about the man who played with himself
between the book stacks while I shelved
Probability and *Image* before closing.
The crickets are not in this poem. Not the summer night,
Pine-Sol mopped over ice-cream-stand floors.
I washed those tiles. This poem does not contain
the spiked punch the fists on the door the
men who circled at the bar and sang,
Just fuck him already. Do us all
a favor. Every year, I write this poem.
I saw them later, passed out drunk
on the carpet when I was pulled into a room.
This poem does not have a mouse.

Not cardinals, not chickadees, not finches.
Every year, I observe pillows and sheets
move into dorms. Yesterday, a boy tried
to take a stick from my daughter's hand. I wouldn't let him.

Empty

New light, new growth, new loss, new sorrow, new joy—this is the condition of spring. I've been thinking about the possibility of emptiness. When something has left, what do we do with the space that the absence makes? In us and in our lives? What if we don't expect something from this state of being and instead notice it, describe it?

This prompt invites you to think about vessels and also about times you've felt like you've been emptied out of yourself.

In your poem on emptiness, you can take this route or you can work with a more Buddhist sensibility, more neutral in your approach (or even tipped toward praise).

1. Jot down six examples of emptiness—things and not abstractions—in your life right now. (An empty object, or a space where something once was are two ways into thinking about this.)

2. Select one of these to focus on by thinking about which one you feel compelled to describe. Don't ask yourself why. Jot down notes about what this emptiness feels like to you, and describe this feeling using concrete details. What color is this emptiness to you? What does it taste like?

3. Jot down notes about what was once in this space or what could be in this space. Describe it as clearly as possible.

4. Jot down a memory that comes to mind for you either about this emptiness or about another emptiness in your life in the past. Why

did you feel empty? How did you respond to this feeling? Was anyone around you when you felt this way? Who? What did they say?

5. Begin your poem with how the emptiness feels to you (notes from step three), and then move into the memory (step four), and then transition into your notes from step two. You might find that shorter lines suit your poem. You're welcome to title your poem by naming the object that was the launchpad for your meditation.

Interlude: Iconostasis of the Former Museum of Atheism

Philip Metres

Образ. Образ. Образ.
These are the faces

staring down our faces.
No cracks will show

their expression
-lessness. Each sacred image

is doom & door. Is wind
& bound to the invisible

precipice. Like a name,
it looms—not you

& yet you. How to rupture
into usable scraps, ritual

to hew
to?

Love in That Place

I have long loved Polish poet Czesław Miłosz's "After Paradise," from his *Collected Poems (1931–1987)*. This particular poem was in his volume *Unattainable Earth*. Fifteen years ago or so, what I loved about this poem was how it captured the feeling of being in love and experiencing a place with a beloved. A city. A garden. A particular afternoon when all things feel possible. My mind did not remember how heteronormative the poem is—or rooted in one kind of desire and idea of gender—and I wish that this poem wasn't this way. I think that when the speaker of Miłosz's poem says, "for the two of you," he means a particular couple—perhaps even the self and a particular beloved in the past.

When I read "After Paradise," its seeming simplicity of diction and occasion fool me every time. "How perfect / All things are" the speaker says (2–3). Oh, come on, grouchy and tired me of the present moment thinks at first. And yet—and yet. That voice captures the way a perfect day can feel, all the while destabilizing this with a single word ringing through the line like a spoon clinking against a teacup: "Now." Now—as though this moment were already passing. This isn't paradise, it is after. This is a moment in the mind that the speaker returns to, and wishes the "you" will return to, in order to hold what might have passed or what could pass in memory.

I encourage you to read Thomas March's "Room 360" and think about it this way, too. How does this love poem interact with place—as memory?

So all of this is to say that I'm encouraging you to write a love poem. Do this by writing about a particular place: a city, a garden, a restaurant, a natural landscape. Speak to the self and the beloved in the past as "you." Let details of the place reveal the tone of the poem. Ambiguity is welcome in your love poem. Your poem can be ambiguous in its relationship to its subject—the idea of a love poem itself!

As I like to remind you, try brainstorming the ideas for this poem with a pen or pencil on paper before turning to the computer. Let go of the inner critic that might try to interrupt you. Your ideas are good. Invite in what comes, and don't self-edit while you are creating. You can prune later.

1. Think about places you've been with a beloved or beloveds—from the past or from your life now. (You're welcome to jot down a few if you like.) Think about places you've meandered, places you've lingered. This can be a café, a garden, a park, a natural landscape, or a city.

2. Choose one beloved and corresponding place, and jot down as many details as you can about the place in a specific moment of time. Think about the weather, the light, what it smelled like, what it sounded like, who or what was there (animals or plants?). If you can't quite remember, you can google this place and refresh your memory through research. You can also imagine what would have been there then.

3. Write a poem to the past self and the beloved that only gives details of the place—not what happened to the relationship. Try to write a love poem about what the place offered or taught the "you" about love. You are welcome to wrestle with what a love poem is or what it means to write about love. Try to let the place carry the feeling that the speaker has about the past self. This feeling can change from moment to moment in the poem.

Room 360

Thomas March

> *Paris, IXe Arrondissement*
> *L'Hôtel R de Paris*
> *2017–*

Again the late light of August—again
Paris and this room, just as we left it,
are new again. We could believe no one
else has slept here since we last closed the door
on this other life that is ours alone.
We reenact our claims on the mattress—
who gets to be closer to the bathroom
and who feels the first breeze from the window.
Cash comingles on the mantle—we share
a closet again, combining our clothes
as we used to. We wear our black and white
tight t-shirts, jeans, and simple shoes—we are
not here to make a show of being here,
breaking out in wide American smiles.
The first few days, we wear out the clichés—
cafés, cathedrals, and couture; Montmartre
to Montparnasse; Poissy to Père Lachaise.
We widen our familiarity
until what remains is just a city
to rediscover as itself—knowing
all cities have been ugly once—as we
have not always been kind to each other.
But we always find comfort in the warmth
of Parisian formality, in streets
made for shadows, just off the boulevards,
and in bed, eating McDonald's again

before dawn, smelling of grease and Hermès.
Tomorrow, walk me once more to the grave
of Oscar Wilde, and we'll pray for us all
and the time to reclaim this life—again.

Large Short Poem

No poem wants to be small! Stanley Plumly, one of my poetry teachers, would say. Part of what he meant was that shorter poems must feel like big poems. When you are reading a poem that occurs as a brief vocal utterance, a meditation that takes up less time to experience, the language itself should feel large. As a reader/listener/perceiver/audience member, you will feel enfolded in the poem and its world.

What does it mean to write a short poem?

As a rambler myself, I have been thinking about this quite a bit, as I tend to wander, meander, and fold tangents and adjectival ornaments into my poems. (I do love working this way, and if you do too, I say *YES*, more, more, more!) But what does it mean to strive to write a large *short* poem? Here, I'm thinking about a poem shorter than fourteen lines because sonnets are fourteen lines; to me, stepping back from the sonnet as a vessel for a poem represents a decision to align with brief, heightened modes of speech. Writing a poem shorter than fourteen lines means committing in that particular poem to a lyricism that takes less time than the song that a sonnet offers the ear.

In a manuscript, a Large Short Poem can be a resting place for a reader between sections. It can also be a way for a poem to shift to a different register of feeling from what came before.

Here are some things that I have been thinking about when approaching Large Short Poems:

- A Large Short Poem moves swiftly through place; the scene is often not one single place (mythic or real), but perhaps at least two imagined spaces the speaker moves through, even from line to line. *If a Large Short Poem focuses on one scene, the speaker could be in motion in it.*

- A Large Short Poem can activate simile—the comparison of two unlike things using like or as—to suggest a physical place and also set up a sweeping shift that the poem will make, most often from one register of feeling to another.

- A Large Short Poem broadens a small observation into a large emotional subject.

- A Large Short Poem might feel like a voice in the ear—something someone says privately to you, something that might feel warm emotionally and contain fewer adjectives so as to convey an immediacy of speech that is almost breathless.

- A Large Short Poem *may* use a choral "We" or switch swiftly from an "I" to a "you." In other words, a Large Short Poem might use first person plural or switch from first person to second swiftly.

- A Large Short Poem is often only a single sentence (perhaps two).

Notice what happens in Ted Kooser's incredible short poem, "A Sunrise without Clouds." How does the initial simile prepare us for the sweeping movement of mind at the end of the poem?

1. Imagine a place where you had a tough decision to make. What did you wish for the most in that moment? Jot this down.

2. In another version of events, what could have happened instead? Jot this down.

3. Begin a poem with "In memory, I…" and recall the place and wish of step one, then move to the other version of events in step two. Add a color to your poem. Try to switch from first person ("I") to second person ("you"). Try to end with a question.

4. The poem should be shorter than fourteen lines. Aim for a single sentence. Your title can add context clues such as place or time. (Did you end up with more than fourteen lines? Aim for two separate Large Short Poems!)

A Sunrise without Clouds

Ted Kooser

It's like a clean kitchen, isn't it…
nearly all gleaming white,

with a lightly-scorched tea-kettle
on a back burner. How very

uninviting a day. I much prefer
those after-a-rain mornings

with enormous lasagnas of clouds
put together the evening before—

ripply noodles, lots of tomato sauce—
left out all night on the counter.

Memory, Body, Elegy

This prompt tangles with and reclaims the bleak, the visceral, the messy. This poem invites the mood of darkness, of the body and all its gore and visceral elements, and of the ways winter can invite goodbyes. A goodbye to light. A goodbye to the year. A goodbye perhaps to a person.

Freewrite about bleak autumn or winter scenes that come to mind: three descriptions of any autumn or winter scene you have experienced. I recall boiling water in my thrift-store spaghetti pot, bringing it outside my apartment, and using it to slowly, pot by pot, melt the ice off the wheels of my frozen car. Bleak, yes! On my list it would go.

Then freewrite about ways that the body has challenged you, discouraged you, or done something other than what you wanted.

Jot down three kinds of material that you'd like to bring into the poem (foam, paper, steel, etc.).

Now that you have your notes, begin the poem with a goodbye of some kind and incorporate your notes. Invite your poem to travel. During the poem's journey, is there a way for the speaker to, in the midst of it all, praise the self for a choice, an action, a promise, or a goal?

American Pastoral

Traci Brimhall

Here, September is already letting go,
       the blond corn shedding, skin curling
off the apple at the knife's slow turn.
       A church sign admonishes, *Take*

your daily walk with the Lord, while out here,
       squirrels persist in saving what they can.
Bears ravage blackberries and chestnuts.
       Schooners take the last good wind around

the Apostle Islands. Stay awake, I'm trying
       to tell you something. Everything begins
with a story. Begin here, where the wolves'
       coats are thickening. Begin at autumn's

bright return, when the late swallowtail
       eats its way out of its old body and heads south.
Where a stone dreams of being and breaks
       out of the mountain. Where power lines sag

with the weight of angels. One rises to eat
       the dead at the roadside, weeping at the strange
birth of flies and the doe's eyes radiant
       with suffering, her body offered to the hungry.

Only the dead let you touch them this way.
       The angel wants more of this. More
generosity. More tenderness. It wants more
       of everything on earth it cannot have.

The Unexpectedly Lit Branch

When you're walking under a tree, have you ever looked up and marveled at an unexpectedly lit branch? The way the sun catches a single limb, or perhaps a few limbs—edging them gold, taking them out of context? Sometimes a branch looks glittery and sharp when caught in the light this way, doesn't it?

How might an offset line—a line set apart from the rest of the poem by being spaced so far to the right of the general distance of line endings—stretch and stretch the length of the right margin in what feels like a momentary expansion? How might this "unexpectedly lit branch" in the tree of your poem offer a way for an image or phrase to gather additional resonance? To sharpen in meaning and emotional register in contrast or conversation with what is happening around that line?

1. Think about objects that your older relatives (grandparent, great-aunt, great-uncle) or family friends/acquaintances gave or showed you as a child—objects that bring up tactile memories. (What can you still almost touch or smell?) Jot down a list of four of these objects and perhaps even where a grandparent shared one.

2. Which object lingers in your mind the most right now? Jot it down. Jot down what about this object sticks with you right now—for whatever reason. (Don't overthink this.)

3. Name a color associated with this object in some way.

4. Jot down what you wished you knew better when you held or touched this object.

5. Begin your poem describing what this period in time felt like for you and then include your description of the object—its details, its color—and allow into your poem what comes. A brief scene might appear in your mind, and you're welcome to include what you like from it in your poem. Make sure to include info from step four. Think about which little details or word clusters might catch the sunlight and stand apart from the poem. You can push the return key and then the tab key and see what happens when you move this word or word cluster farther and farther to the right margin. Try to do this three or four times, perhaps more, but no more than six.

Tip: You might find yourself playing with stanzas that are different lengths. If you do, try to include at least one couplet in your poem.

Testament

Eugenia Leigh

A small woman lives in a flowerpot in my closet.
She hates light. Brandishes her fists
                              when she speaks. Not speaks—

mocks. She asks about my parents: *tell me a tragedy.*
I've practiced that tragedy.
But *this* is the truth:

I never feared him. I feared *her*—her radiance, her hymns.

My fear being   resistance to the impossible.
The impossible,   a woman who endured.

He never said one kind word to her.
My father, I mean. To my mother, I mean.

Where did she gather those   *You are beautiful*s
for my sisters and me?   How did she never empty of warmth?

The small woman in the flowerpot loathes
my mother's clean, clean bones.

She once dared me to spit in my mother's face.
                              (She didn't spit back.)

When I was fifteen,   my mother found me
in a bookstore with a boy   pressed against my body—his muscles,

his jaw. I *let* him mark me.
        After years of raking her bruises
                away from her daughters, *that* was the only night
                              my mother let me see her cry.

When God passed out mothers to all the beastly children
and wives to all the beasts,
how did he misplace my mother in that wrong pile?

And yet, her devastating joy.   That rosy voice
insisting, insisting   God *is* good.

On Lilacs and Desire

T. S. Eliot famously said, "April is the cruelest month"—well, the speaker of his poem, "The Wasteland" said this—and every year, I both want to roll my eyes at this statement whenever I hear it quoted out of context *and* on a cold, rainy day nod my head and say, *OK, fine. I can agree.*

I want to look again at "The Wasteland," a poem that I first remember encountering as a freshman in college in a poetry survey course *and* a poem that I have taught many times in such courses at different universities. It's strange, marvelous, funny, dark. Troubled, troubling in all of its Modernist fragments. The full passage that "April is the cruelest month" comes from is as follows:

> April is the cruelest month, breeding
> Lilacs out of the dead land, mixing
> Memory and desire, stirring
> Dull roots with spring rain. (1–4)

What I want to think about are these lilacs. The earth, which has seemed "dead," now offers these purple flowers with a scent that is lovely and demanding. I just love the smell of lilacs, and I also find myself thinking that the olfactory senses are invited to a multilayered experience when you put your nose to one. There's the sweetness, and then there's this almost wet, woody smell. A kind of heaviness. The flowers seem to carry with them their journey through death as they offer beauty, change, and a spot of color in the dirt.

I've been finding joy in the flowers I spot in my neighborhood—yellows, reds, purples in fenced-off plots, in pots on steps, cut and bunched in plastic vessels. I want to look at the phrase from Eliot's poem, "mixing / memory and desire." Each flower carries the story of its growth inside of its journey as it blooms. In a way, when we are creating visual images, we, too, are "mixing / memory and desire": our relationship with the thing connects with what we want it to communicate and how we want to possess it in language.

1. Think of flowers you have smelled and very specific places you have smelled them. The first time you smelled a rose, a lilac, a lily? Where were you? Who was with you? Jot down details that come to mind.

2. Think more about this memory, and add three colors to it and one smell in addition to the scent of the flower.

3. What was a secret you carried inside of you at this moment, in this memory? (It can be anything, big or small—something about how your name was said, something about your hunger, something about what you wanted to say.)

4. Begin a poem by speaking to the "you" of the past using your notes to guide you. Address this "you" through the second person: "You stood.... You wondered.... You wished...." Begin in the memory.

5. As the poem unfolds, think about what you want now. Can you add this in with the statement, "What I want now is..."

Tip: Let your poem unfurl. When you are ready to revise it, you might find that quatrains (four-line stanzas) become a vase that supports the mixing of memory and desire your poem invites.

from "The Waste Land"

T. S. Eliot

I. The Burial of the Dead

April is the cruellest month, breeding
Lilacs out of the dead land, mixing
Memory and desire, stirring
Dull roots with spring rain.
Winter kept us warm, covering
Earth in forgetful snow, feeding
A little life with dried tubers.
Summer surprised us, coming over the Starnbergersee
With a shower of rain; we stopped in the colonnade,
And went on in sunlight, into the Hofgarten,
And drank coffee, and talked for an hour.
Bin gar keine Russin, stamm' aus Litauen, echt deutsch.
And when we were children, staying at the archduke's,
My cousin's, he took me out on a sled,
And I was frightened. He said, Marie,
Marie, hold on tight. And down we went.
In the mountains, there you feel free.
I read, much of the night, and go south in the winter.

What are the roots that clutch, what branches grow
Out of this stony rubbish? Son of man,
You cannot say, or guess, for you know only
A heap of broken images, where the sun beats,
And the dead tree gives no shelter, the cricket no relief,
And the dry stone no sound of water. Only
There is shadow under this red rock,
(Come in under the shadow of this red rock),
And I will show you something different from either
Your shadow at morning striding behind you
Or your shadow at evening rising to meet you;
I will show you fear in a handful of dust.

On Lilacs and Desire

Rooms for the Party

Write a poem in quatrains where you think of each four-line stanza as a room for the party that you're throwing inside of it. This writing exercise has two parts.

1. Freewrite (just put down a paragraph!) about the following things:

- Choose a body part (finger, arm, eye, etc.)

- Choose a mood (anger, praise, gratitude, etc.)

- What do you want to do the most right now?

- Can you include colors and textures?

You're shopping and thinking about your invitations. Don't worry at all about form.

2. Creating the space! Your quatrain party can be a party for the self, it can have a group of people, one other person—whatever you want!

Your stanza boundaries are yours to shape.

Begin to shape your writing exercise into four-line stanzas. As you do this, consider decorations (vivid descriptions and actions), people (I, you, we, or characters), food and music (what you're doing at the party, or what is happening in the stanza), and games (any wordplay or repetition you might like to engage).

Tip: Not every stanza needs wordplay! You can think about which one or ones might benefit from some.

He Has an Oral Fixation

Natalie Scenters-Zapico

He can't stop putting the dead
flowers, the deadhead nails, the dead weight
sacks of flour, in his mouth. He can't
stop writing about the mouth. The way

he woke up to his mouth full of bees,
their dead crunch still stinging
his gums. He writes: *There's something*
beautiful in the way a mouth can be broken

by saliva & cold air. She broke
his mouth open & filled it with lead-
tainted earth. She made him
brain-dead through the mouth;

licked the honey she pulled
from his incisors like sap from a tree.
His mouth, with its stretch marks
running along his cheeks — she's never seen

anything like it. His mouth a scar
of his hunger, a scar of his gluttony
after the hunger. Stop writing
about the mouth: the teeth, the gums,

the impacted tooth & its psychedelic
blues and greens. Stop writing how she bit
your mouth & with a blowtorch
welded its dark-open shut. Stop writing

about the mouth: the tongue, the holy
molars, the wear of grinding yourself
to bone. Stop writing about the mouth:
his mouth, your mouth, her mouth.

From a Distance

Write a poem addressed to someone in your life who you have not seen in at least six months or someone you could not see during a period of quarantine *or* about something particular—individual to you—that you've experienced in isolation. What were things you would have said to someone that you could only say in person? Try to include at least one question in your poem. This can be a poem of any length.

Matzoh

Gail Mazur

As if to mock me in my widowhood
as if to deny my pandemic isolation
this huge carton arrives at my door,
an absurd cosmic mistake from Yehuda
Matzos: ten boxes, which should last
long enough to get incinerated
with me at the old New England
cemetery that was once the family
farm of poet Robert Creeley's greatgrandfather,
and where his descendants
can be buried together ad aeternam.
Mirabile dictu, that Bob and the ashes
of my beloved—and mine—will lie in
that pastoral landscape where I like to
walk on spring mornings. One of the first
arboreal cemeteries, a sanctuary, really,
for mourners, bird watchers, and my friends
the Sunday botanizers. Should I be buried—
or should my ashes just be sprinkled about
with old dry crumbs of Yehuda's uncalledfor
unrisen bread? Such questions never
occurred in what today we call "normal times"
when I'd bring cut flowers to lay on our stone
etched with a palette, a brush, a pen, nestled
alongside the markers of other Jews,
and Chinese and Armenians, near Malamud
and Achilles Fang and Izzy Stone, far
from Longfellow and Mary Baker Eddy,
overlooking a pond which is serene home
all summer to a picturesque pair of
weeping willows and two white swans.

Who was the misinformed deliverer of
such excess to my door, of these symbols
of my people's eternal hardships? O
Yehuda Matzos, Yehuda Matzos, yes,
in your crisp hard plenitude you mock
and (kind of) amuse me, when I'd forgotten
how you've always been baked
with the salty tears of my people's exodus—
but oh, I will eat, and eat alone, until the day
I can eat no more of our unleavened bread.

Sonnet Yourself

Let's think about sonnets. Courtly love, subversive relationships, time-wrecked joy, and a deep reckoning with the contemporary *you*—the ever-present self is revealed and concealed in the poem. The sonnet became Petrarch's form in Italy in the fourteenth century and then Shakespeare's in England in the early seventeenth century. And let's not forget Wanda Coleman's American sonnets, a fantastic contemporary take on the hundreds-of-years-old form.

At its core, the sonnet is a fourteen-line sound machine that pumps with your blood and breath. You might recall the Shakespearian ABABCDCDEFE-FGG rhyme scheme. You might have tapped out the five-beat rhythmic pattern of iambic pentameter—unstressed and stressed syllables—on a desk or your knee. You might remember that the sonnet has a volta, or turn, that spins its argument on its axis.

In conversation with Diane Seuss's unrhymed sonnets, I invite you to write your own unrhymed sonnet (no rhyme scheme, no meter!). I invite you to *sonnet yourself*: to craft an "I" that does whatever the hell you want it to in the span of fourteen lines. You'll wrangle with an idea, a memory, a concept, a quote, or a mix of any and all of these things as you think about what love is and means in all of its beauty and tragedy.

In sonneting yourself, you can write about anything you want. You can make the sonnet yours.

1. What book is on your nightstand? (Or books, if you're like me and there's a pile waiting for you?) Choose one, flip through it, and find a quote that grabs you. Jot your quote down.

2. Who was your first crush? What was it about this person that flipped your world upside down? Jot down five details, and try to include scents and colors if you can.

3. If you could do anything in the world right now—this instant—no matter how big or small, what would it be? Don't overthink this! Jot down the first thing that comes to mind.

4. What would the you of today say to the you who had the crush? This can be anything.

5. Go to a cupboard in your kitchen or another room in your home. What thing inside catches your eye? Jot this down.

6. You're ready to begin your poem. You're aiming for fourteen lines, but if you are a few long or short, you can tweak your poem after it's drafted to get it to fourteen. Begin either with the quote from step one or the thing that you want to do right now in step three. Then weave in the details—as many as you can—from the other parts of your brainstorming activity. As you write, try to repeat a phrase twice. You can pick any phrase you choose, but here are some suggestions: "I thought I'd…" "I couldn't wait…" "I kicked…" "I left…" As you near the end of your poem, try to add something that changes the mood, pace, or subject.

Tip: Let the energy of the poem carry you. Trim or expand it to get to fourteen lines.

Sonnet 130

William Shakespeare

My mistress' eyes are nothing like the sun;
Coral is far more red than her lips' red;
If snow be white, why then her breasts are dun;
If hairs be wires, black wires grow on her head.
I have seen roses damask'd, red and white,
But no such roses see I in her cheeks;
And in some perfumes is there more delight
Than in the breath that from my mistress reeks.
I love to hear her speak, yet well I know
That music hath a far more pleasing sound;
I grant I never saw a goddess go;
My mistress, when she walks, treads on the ground:
    And yet, by heaven, I think my love as rare
    As any she belied with false compare.

American Sonnet 18

Wanda Coleman

> *—after June Jordan*

this is the place where all the lives
are planted in my eyes. black things writhe
on the ground. red things gush from
volcanic gaseous tremblings/become blood and light
mountains of flesh raging toward rapturous seas
where crowns of trees inspired by flame extol the night

(my abysmal hear compels the moon compels
wave upon wave. compels reason)

the tombs are fertile with sacred
rememberings. the ancient rhymes. the
disasters of couplings. the turbulent blaze of
greed's agonies. shadows reaching for time and time
unraveling and undone.

sky river mother—your tongue plunders my mouth

[Either all of this is an apparition or I am]

Diane Seuss

Either all of this is an apparition or I am, and where the apparition

began I don't rightly know, maybe I'm still coupled, maybe I have

a towhead in tow, my singularity in every circumstance a mirage,

reading *Dubliners* at Orlando's eating a taco while the whole

world sips its margaritas in tandem, watching a meteor shower

from a blue picnic table in the dark near a tributary of the Rio

Grande, wild dogs rambling through the pueblo beneath the Blood

of Christ mountains where I will never belong nor should I,

and magpies with the indigo feathers down their backs

who can recognize their own faces in looking glasses, or Intro

to Buddhism, peyote-tripping through class, the prof spinning

a prayer wheel like a party favor, maybe all the way back to being

trapped with my dad in a House of Mirrors, reaching for a father

and banging into glass, self, self, impairment, hallucination

Facing Down the Poem

I invite you to face down another poem and imagine yourself inside of it. Tangling with it. Maybe even celebrating it while you wrestle with it. To prepare for this prompt, I encourage you to think about a poem from another time, maybe even a poem you've studied in an anthology or class. (Feel free to go to your bookshelf and browse!)

The speaker of Rebecca Hazelton's "Sexy is the Least Interesting" faces down another poem, Allen Ginsberg's famous "A Supermarket in California" (I encourage you to google it!) The speaker of Ginsberg's poem proclaims, "What peaches and what penumbras! Whole families shopping at night!" (Ginsberg's speaker is, in turn, imagining having an erotic encounter with another poet of a previous era, Walt Whitman.) The speaker of Hazelton's poem responds to this moment of Ginsberg's poem, nodding to the conceit of Ginsberg's poem while also tangling with its marvel and what might lie within it:

> —I must confess, Allen G,
> that the stacked peaches are more fuzz for me than flesh
> these days, the eggplants less turgid, swelling gleam
> than a problem of use. (6–9)

How might you address a former poet—or even a moment of a former poet's poem? How might this invite you to think about something special that you can do in your own poem?

1. Think about poems that you've studied in a class or have encountered on your own, poems that you love or have always wanted to tangle with. Make a brief list (three poems). As you do, think about the

assumptions the speaker makes, the proclamations, or the poem's setting itself.

2. Consider which poem on your list sticks with you the most right now. It might be that you have always loved it, or you never quite got it, or you wondered why the speaker made the choices they did. Or maybe you don't know why this poem is sticking with you, and that's OK. Circle or underline whichever poem from your list you can't get out of your head.

3. Now that you've chosen your poem, make notes about what the speaker of that poem is doing, which might be quite different from your own experience. Jot down what you might do instead, in a similar situation. (Or, say why you haven't been in the same situation as this speaker.) Redescribe one thing in the poem you've chosen in your own words, using a simile or metaphor.

4. What does the speaker proclaim or say in the poem you've chosen? Think of one key statement/utterance. What question would you ask the speaker of that poem about why they've said what they did?

5. Now, think about the setting or scene of the poem. Where does the poem take place? How is your own situation/setting different? Why? Describe a scene from your life with vivid detail and use at least two colors and two textures.

6. Now you're ready to begin. Start in the scene itself—the scene of your life—and make this as real as possible. Fold in the details brainstormed in step 5. Then bring in the poet whose work you're facing down; include details from steps three and four. Notice the mood or tone of your poem, and as you write, describe the speaker's scene in a way that captures that mood as best as you can. Try writing in either longer lines or shorter lines than you're used to.

Bonus: Include three or four rhyming words that you embed within the lines of your poem.

Sexy Is the Least Interesting

Rebecca Hazelton

thing I do, but it's the thing I've done the most,
and now that I can glide through a supermarket

without a stock boy's notice, now that I am
indistinguishable from the day-olds and the must-gos

and the bend of my waist above the cheese bin
brings not a one to their knees—I must confess, Allen G,

that the stacked peaches are more fuzz for me than flesh
these days, the eggplants less turgid, swelling gleam

than a problem of use. In the dream of the produce aisle,
all was emoji. The carts slid inside the other carts

without a hitch. The bins held their contents tightly.
All was desire and surplus—once I touched

a cellophaned cube of meat and felt it gently give
beneath the pressure. I was a woman who left a mark.

I lived dangerously. Now the store detective marks me
as yet another white, suburban mother. My God, Allen,

yesterday I shoplifted a turkey and no one noticed. I wish I could
close my eyes and see you on aisle C17 once more—

Speak to me again of out-of-season
asparagus—the girth of them—I want to feel

the parsnips thick beneath my hand, I want to bite
the sliced orange sample and let the juice drip, and see

another person's eyes gaze hungrily.
Allen, I have been considering the cost of things

and ideas. Allen, my queer shoulder is bared
in an off-the-shoulder sweatshirt.

Above the lettuce, false lightning
and simulated thunder. Tinny Gene Kelly

sings out about rain and joy from across the century,
and the mist that sprays does not spray for me.

Moving through
Story, Movie, Myth

You're the Director Now

What was the last film or TV show that you watched? Which character do you either identify with a lot or not at all?

1. Imagine that you are writing instructions for that particular character in a scene where they were. What do you want them to do differently? Now imagine that the character is in a completely new location—perhaps even a dream that you recently had. What do they do that you are not in favor of? What worries you about them? Jot down your answers to these questions.

2. In this exploration, your poem acts like the voice of a director in that you will try not to use the "I" at all; describe the actions and then tell the character to do things (Stop, Go here, Go there). If you use the "I," try to use it only once or twice. If you talk to the character, does the character listen? What is at stake for them, and for you, in telling this story? Incorporate your notes and ideas from step one. Aim for a longer poem in this draft; you might even find that this exploration will produce a prose poem (a poem without line breaks) that you then trim and shape into a shorter poem.

I Want to Be Stark[Like]

Leah Umansky

Game of Thrones

A man is only worth what people say he is
and those Starks are good stock. They'll knee-deep it.
They famish the craving they are fathered by.
Manning the forestry of life, they are steadfast and sturdy.

When pungent or cruel, they sauce the ache.
Light folds them in two.
What I want to say is, *I would meet you upon this.*

Let me, too, carry the token of the world.
Tell me the secret of what comes next,
and then take me

river   river   river

Dreaming the Animal

Do you remember your dreams so clearly that you feel like you've just seen a (strange!) movie when you open your eyes? Or do you wake up recalling only one clear image or action? Or do you find that you don't often remember your dreams but that there's a recurring place or object that appears to you from time to time?

Once in a while, I'll have a dream that's so vivid I wish I wrote it down before it slips away. However, I do dream of a few recurring themes or places. Sometimes, I'm lost in an airport, for example.

This poem invites you to think about one thing in a dream landscape that is recent or recurring. You can consider one thing that is *quotidian*, one thing that is from everyday life that you wouldn't be surprised to encounter on a regular day. Or you can consider something extraordinary, not tied to the real, something distinctly part of the logic of the dream. Or you can consider a place that you've dreamed about.

In any case, the goal for this poem is for you to describe what you've chosen as crisply as possible so it *feels* like it's part of our lived world.

1. Brainstorm some dreams you've had recently. If your mind goes blank at this, you're welcome to sit with a piece of paper and pen and write "I don't remember my dreams because" and then see what comes up. You might find yourself remembering a dream (or nightmare) from your childhood. Or you might find yourself coming up with a recurring place you've dreamed about. Or an object. Or animal. Jot down four different dream elements (objects, places, animals) that you can recall.

2. Come up with six colors and list them, but when you do this, try to connect these colors to objects, flowers, animals, or foods. (Lemon yellow, granite gray, etc.)

3. Now think about the list from step one. Which dream image sticks with you the most right now? Don't ask yourself why! Just underline or circle it.

4. Begin your poem by describing your image/place/object as crisply and specifically as possible. You're welcome to state that this is not a real thing. Or that it *is* a real thing. You're welcome to inspect the image as the speaker of the poem. To be detached. To ask questions. To be skeptical. As you write, I'd like you to add the colors from step two. Then, if you have not included an animal, think about if there were an animal (or bird) in the dream space you're writing about—or in connection with the dream object or image—which animal would it be? Can your poem include this animal/bird? Or speak about its absence from this dream space? Let your poem take you where it goes. Can your poem's speaker become more and more immersed in the dreamscape that you've created?

Bonus: Try your poem without stanza breaks or in quatrains (four-line stanzas).

Joy

Miller Oberman

Like the time I dreamt about a loon family,
just some common loons—not metaphors
in any way, just real loons in a lake swimming
near each other so it was clear they were a set,
preferring each other's company in the cold
still lake with its depth of reflected pines.
The curve of their black heads and sleek
necks, black and white stripes then checks
on their folded wings, floating so low
atop their reflections they almost seem
inside them. Their wails like wolves, their
calls like an echo without origin, their
calls like an echo of lake, or what makes lake
lake. How nice to think the male and female
loons cannot be told apart by their plumage
and that they build a nest and sit on eggs
together. One of their calls is called "tremolo."

The Big Reveal

The goal of this poem is to enact a big reveal where key information within the story (narrative, emotional, or both) the poem tells is delayed until the ending. You can imagine this to be like a mystery, in a sense, where all is unveiled at the end of the poem. In Beth Ann Fennelly's "Two Sisters...," we don't know the full story about the sister until the very end of the poem, for example.

1.   Brainstorm memories or situations where you have felt very angry at someone—or jealous, or sad, or lonely—as well as the location where this feeling took place. What happened? Try to come up with two or three ideas, and for each one jot down details about the place where this happened as well as what happened.

2.   Choose a situation and think about it: what happened and why? Jot down notes for yourself. Now, choose one crucial fact or part of the event to keep hidden from the reader.

3.   Think about two colors and one sound you want to include in your poem. Be as vivid as possible.

4.   Begin your poem as though you are telling a story, in as grounded a voice as possible (though you're welcome to shift the poem's emotional register as you get going if you like). Work the colors you chose, as well as the sound, into your poem. Describe the scene/place where the anger, rage, or sadness happened, and offer as many details as you can—except for details that clue the reader into the information you're choosing not to reveal. Let your mind wander. If

your poem shifts into a new place, a new scene, or even adds another character, let this happen.

5. At the end of your poem, reveal the thing that you have kept hidden. You are welcome to do this along with a shift in address (the speaker can speak to a "you" directly or summon a "we").

Tip: If you're stuck, you can describe a movie you've seen where you imagine yourself or another person to be one of the characters, and you can open up the plot and relate it to your own life.

Two Sisters, One Thinner, One Better Dressed

Beth Ann Fennelly

When my sister and I would meet at her apartment before heading out to bars, I would choose my clothes with care. I knew that when I walked through her door, she would study me, especially if a few weeks or more had passed since we'd seen each other. Sisters are envious, sure, but we were also information gathering. We looked a bit alike, so it was a way to test how we'd fare in a different outfit, haircut. She was often thinner than I was, but I had better style. Younger by two years, I was her leader only in fashion; I would often be wearing something she hadn't considered yet. She would ask me where I got it, and I would tell her, maybe showing off a little. Sometimes she'd want to try it on and I would accessorize her, cuff her jeans or angle the belt correctly on her hips. If she asked, we'd swap outfits for the night. It was worth being the frumpier one to make her happy.

I'm still aware of how I look when I visit her. I live in a different state now, so it's not as often, but when I'm back in Illinois at our mom's house, I always end my run by visiting her. I stand panting in the grass at my sister's feet. I'm aware of how she sees me, huffing clouds from my lungs, my legs strong, my skin bright with sweat in my new running clothes. Still showing off, I suppose, as she's stuck wearing the navy suit I chose the last time I styled her, a suit now thirteen years outdated, though fashionable enough when they closed the casket.

Traveling through the Tale

Think about mythical stories and fairy tales that interest you. (You're welcome to refresh your memory by doing some googling and broaden your knowledge!) You can also incorporate religious stories, if you like.

1. Think about a mythical story or fairy tale, and choose a character that is not the focal point of the story. In other words, ask yourself who else is in the story besides the main character.

2. What does this character see and hear? How do they feel about their predicament? What could they do to be the main character of the story? Jot down notes.

3. Choose this minor character from a mythical tale and write a poem from their point of view, exploring these questions, but set the story in the present day. Think about how they travel in their story or even could travel away from their predicament. Try to incorporate as many colors in your poem as you can.

Bedtime Story: Part 1 (Gretel)

Lauren K. Alleyne

There was no way back—
the birds had pecked our loaf to nothing
our small hearts in their beaks;
we wandered the dark, despairing.

Then, the tiniest whiff—
honey and ginger and cinnamon—
the sweetest ache. We ran towards
what our noses thought was home.

The stories call her a witch,
but she was our third mother,
our private, tragic joke. We told
her of our mother's passing,

our father's slide into madness,
how step-mother lulled him into calm,
or made her small body its own defiant storm,
how she sent us out, and didn't look back.

I will be your third mother, she said,
and we bowed our heads, ashamed
to have run through so many mothers;
afraid she meant stepmother was gone too.

She must have read the look on us,
(her only witchery) and said, *Come
now, I'm too young to be called Grandmother,
call me Nenny!* And we did, shyly,

the syllables tripping awkwardly at first,
growing surer with each passing day.
She fed us milk and bread (so much
like step-mother's heavy loaves!);

She taught us the wood—
the berries and roots that would satisfy
hunger and thirst; how to make a fire
from stones and breath—lessons in survival.

But we saw she would not survive
the waiting. Days into weeks into months,
and still, no step-mother. We saw
how her smile brittled, grief tuning her

voice to an unfamiliar timbre,
how her eyes measured us when she thought
we weren't looking. We saw
the storm gathering in her, and made ready.

One morning, we found her
asleep in her chair beside the oven.
We wept as we fed her body
to the flames, huddled against her final warmth

until the air was heavy with ash.
We bundled ourselves, packed
food, potions—a small inheritance—
and headed out into the motherless dark.

Music Floating Through

As I sit down to write this prompt, I can hear the hum of my neighbor's music through the wall. I'm not annoyed—I like catching what it is. My window is open, and along with the sound of ambient noise (cars, voices, dogs barking, the rustling of wind through the trees), I can also hear an indiscernible humming. Bass. Drums. *Something.*

Music, in one way or another, is so often a backdrop for other things happening in our lives, isn't it? When you were in sixth grade, what song was playing on the radio? What lyrics did you hear floating out of a car window as it drove by? What glimmers of sound—guitar, drums—could you pick up on at different points in your life? Or, more recently, what have you been listening to while you're going through love, pain, boredom, anger, or joy? Hanif Abdurraqib's "Carly Rae Jepsen – "E•MO•TION" captures the feeling of listening to Carly Rae Jepsen's *Emotion* album with an electrifying energy.

Close your eyes and think about bands you listened to or heard on the radio when you were in your teens or early twenties. Where did you hear music—a bus, a car, the radio, a stereo? Maybe you heard a band perform live? Maybe someone hummed or belted out the lyrics to a Top 40 hit? What have you heard recently, either intentionally or accidentally? Let your mind wander before you write anything down.

1. After giving yourself the space to float through the past, jot down specific songs you remember hearing. (You can use the internet to help you recall the full title or band name, if you need to. Just set a timer so you don't fall into a Google rabbit hole!). Try to come up with four songs.

2. Now that you have four songs, jot down a brief description of where you most vividly remember hearing each song floating by—even a fragment of it.

3. Think about the scents and colors that come to mind from the memory of the songs you jotted down. Which memory stands out to you the most right now? Choose this song and memory for your poem.

4. Jot down two lyrics from this song. Jot down notes about anyone you were with in your memory of the song. Write down a place where you heard or even thought of this song recently.

5. Begin your poem in the present—today—and what this song sounds like to you now. Use at least two similes and try to incorporate a texture or a color into your similes. As you write, blend the past with the present, and describe the exact scene where you remember hearing a fragment of the song. What did you feel like? Why? Who was with you? How do you feel now? Switch back and forth from the past to the present in your poem, if you can. You can try talking to your past self as "you" if you'd like to. End your poem by describing one sound from the song *or* one vivid detail from the memory it evokes for you.

Carly Rae Jepsen—"E • MO • TION"
Hanif Abdurraqib

There is more than one way to cover a temple in platinum. Maybe we both long for an era when there were less things to record death. In the interview, they asked if you believe in love at first sight. You said *I think I* have to. You didn't say we are all one hard storm away from dissolving, vanishing *into the frenzied dusk*. But I get it. I know what it is to walk into the mouth of an unfamiliar morning and feel everything. I touch hands with a stranger who gives me my change at the market, and I already know their history. I suppose this is survival. I will love those who no one else thinks to remember. This is all that is promised: there will be a decade you are born, and a decade that you will not make it out of alive. All of the rooftops where the parties were in the year of my becoming are now dust. No one dances so close to the sky anymore. I say *I, too, am a romantic*, and I mean I never expected to survive this long. I have infinite skin. I keep dry when the rain comes. There will always be another era of bright suits that don't quite fit, but must. There will always be a year where the cameras are hungry for whatever sins we can strangle out of the night. There will always be another spoon for boys to lick the sugar from.

Bad Movie

List three movies that trouble you for one reason or another. A plot line you don't buy? A problematic character? A protagonist who just doesn't get it? Write a poem that addresses either a specific character or a specific thing within the setting (a prop!). Tell it! But also try to correct what is wrong with it. Be as specific as you can with colors, shapes, textures. If, while you're brainstorming, ideas about the experience of watching a movie that's "bad," or a blockbuster hit, or a kitschy or campy film come to mind, jot them down. As you write your poem, include these details. But don't say directly how or why the movie isn't working or doing what you wish it would do. Let your descriptions speak instead.

Bonus: Try your poem in quatrains (four-line stanzas) or as a prose poem.

Movie

Dana Levin

EXIT,
     blood-red beacon in the dark.
The screen gray like smoke, gray
     as a scrim of ash,
the red curtains furling round it like flames.
     Red curtains, red walls, red seats and carpet, even our faces
under red-reflected shadows—
     Me and two kids and a man.
Sunny outside, unbearable.
     Sunny,

after five days of rain, the day demanding
     to be entered and filled,
the clouds having dropped from its enormous
     shoulders,
and the duty, to be present for it,
     to say My what a fine summer day...

     The lopped-off fifth of Cinema Five, pinky
masquerading
     as a hand—

     I went in, I waited, for the flashes and burns
of another blockbuster, for the requisite explosions
     and hip bon mots,
for the red aesthetic
     slaughter—

     And the two kids: what did they want?
A little chaos, a little blood
     to make their day, their unpredictable fragmented day—

And the man,
    what did he want?
O long tunnel out of despair, distraction of someone else's
    story—

But the waiting, the silence,
    the red.
Like a dark, like a lullaby—
    like a cave.
Because wasn't there the urge to something sacred in it,
    the cars and kids and hysterical sirens
unable to penetrate
    the air-conditioned vessel where we sprawled or slumped,
mute,
    inviolate, prima materia
for the chemic operations
    of thunder and light in the pitchman's hands, O
Arnold, Disney, Mafia two-step, make us, make us
    be—

something else for awhile.
    Or nothing else for awhile, a series of stunning self-
destructions: point A
    where we slit our throats, point B where the paper shredder
churns us up, and
    C the slash, the cuffs, the gun, all evil bloodied
and done—

    like a dark, like a lullaby—

    to slake the blood-urge to the drum, the dance,
the hypnoid figures made alive in the fire
    of crowding torches
wavering in the stink of the kill—

the spirit in the spirit pictures come—

when there was something there, to lick it all up,
something to pray to, to fear,
       to appease—

It was sunny, unbearable, after five days of rain, I couldn't stand it, the riot
       of good-mornings-so-beautiful, I went
to the movies, my collusion, consolation, twenty minutes early
       before the first bad preview
rated G for its violence and complete lack of sex, rated G
       for us
the general audience, me and two kids and a desolate-looking man,
       we went in,
we waited, for the flashes and burns of the next great escape
       from the tyrannous day
called Thinking and Feeling, in the lopped-off fifth
       of Cinema 5,
the three black blocks on the dark red walls
       a plastic fleur-de-lis—

To give up the burden awhile.
       To be an eye.
Perceiver.
       God of the kingdom.

Getting from Here to There

Brainstorm ways you've travelled from point A to point B in your life: bicycle, car (specific make and model), plane, boat, your own two feet in particular shoes you recall, ferry, motorcycle, skateboard, rollerblade...etc.! Now think one of these means of travel that you like *the least* (or dislike completely) for a particular reason. Danger? Fatigue? Boredom?

1. Research three things you did not know before about this means of travel (enjoy going down a Google rabbit hole!), and jot them down.

2. Now, write a *praise* poem, or ode, in shorter lines than you are used to that begins with *condemning,* or lightly critiquing if that better serves your poem, this means of travel and ends with *praising* it or offering the scene beauty. Incorporate the information you discovered about this means of travel. You might want to incorporate the "you" pronoun at some point in your poem.

Vacation

Rita Dove

I love the hour before takeoff,
that stretch of no time, no home
but the gray vinyl seats linked like
unfolding paper dolls. Soon we shall
be summoned to the gate, soon enough
there'll be the clumsy procedure of row numbers
and perforated stubs—but for now
I can look at these ragtag nuclear families
with their cooing and bickering
or the heeled bachelorette trying
to ignore a baby's wail and the baby's
exhausted mother waiting to be called up early
while the athlete, one monstrous hand
asleep on his duffel bag, listens,
perched like a seal trained for the plunge.
Even the lone executive
who has wandered this far into summer
with his lasered itinerary, briefcase
knocking his knees—even he
has worked for the pleasure of bearing
no more than a scrap of himself
into this hall. He'll dine out, she'll sleep late,
they'll let the sun burn them happy all morning
—a little hope, a little whimsy
before the loudspeaker blurts
and we leap up to become
Flight 828, now boarding at Gate 17.

Strata

Prose poems seem like stories, don't they? On the page, they look like a singular brick, or multiple blocks, of text. However, they skid around corners, they burst with kaleidoscopic imagery—just when a narrative gets off the ground—and they skip forward and backward in time. What prose poems reveal are more than the result of a series of actions a speaker or character takes. Prose poems *are* actions in themselves, as a form: movements of mind.

In telling the story that the speaker seems to explain, the prose poem goes deeper and deeper into experience, into memory, and into the sensory in ways that resist linear meaning. I love this. Sentences can jam next to sentences and create sparks through juxtaposition.

"Ink-Light" is a prose poem in stratified blocks from Natalie Diaz's *Postcolonial Love Poem*. Natalie Diaz focuses on what a lexicon is and can do in different languages as well as image systems in her poems.

I admire the way that the poem ends with action. Burning, breaking, holding.

This prompt is about diving into language and embracing excess. I invite you to let sound guide you, even if you feel that you are moving away from sense. The poem will create its own logic. You will find your way in and out.

1. Make a list of colors—at least four. Be as specific as possible in naming them! *Bonus: Compare one of the colors to a fruit or vegetable.*

2. Think of a very, very cold place you've been. Describe it in as much detail as possible by naming at least one warm thing in your description.

3. Go to a closet in your living space and list five items inside of it. Don't overthink this! Nothing is too little, too seemingly insignificant.

4. Choose a mood: anger, lust, sadness, joy.

5. Write a prose poem where you describe being in the cold space and speak directly to a "you" about the mood you've decided to focus on. Let sound guide you. Write as much as you can without stopping. If you find yourself losing steam, write "No. I will…" and keep going. Incorporate as many of the colors and objects into your prose poem as you can. Get wild. Play. Don't worry about sense.

6. As you reach the end of your poem, write about a time of day: dawn, dusk, noon, late morning. Once you have your giant prose poem block, break it into strata—into paragraphs.

Ink-Light

Natalie Diaz

We move within the snow-chromed world: Like-animal. Like-deer. An
alphabet. Along a street white as lamplight into the winter, walking—: like
language, a new text. I touch her with the eyes of my skin.

The way I read any beloved—: from the ramus of the left jaw down to the
cuneiform of the right foot. She isn't so much what she is—: and becomes
herself only when added to the space where she isn't. What is touch—: not the
touch not the hand but the white heat it floats through.

I count her my desires, mark her—: hoofprints across the frozen page. *Four
strokes of dusk. Carbon black, Lamp black, Bone black, Hide glue*—: I am the
alchemist of ink. She answers me, *Quicksilver,*

and the noise of her boots upon the snow is the weight of a night bird bending
the meteor-blue branch fruiting white flames of cotton. Each of her steps, an
allograph—: bird, flexed limb, perfect line of vertebrae, the glyph of my pelvis.

When I put my teeth to her wrist, the world goes everywhere white. Not sound
but the dizzying nautilus of what is both the palm and the ear. I invented her
hand in this texture—: a grapheme.

In me, a feeling—: white blossom with a red-sided icosahedron inside the
velveteen car of a gold train vibrating the violet tunnel of my throat on its way
to a dimmed station in my chest—: twenty seats of desire, and I am sitting in
each one.

I burn on the silver sparks of her breath moving out of her body. The miracle.
No. The power and the glory glory glory of her—: she breathes. Out—: Out—:
twenty red seats of desire, I break every one. A series of waves against hammer
anvil stirrup—: a vibration of light I can hold with my mouth.

Hike through the Woods

What happens if you explore gaps and spaces purely organically—by feel? How might pauses within the line appear and disappear as though on their own and not tied to a specific approach? I'm imagining this strategy as a "hike through the woods," where you step in and out of sun and shadow that form intricate patterns on your hands and feet from many kinds of trees, light dappling the path before and behind you, such that you're deeply embedded in the place where light is appearing and disappearing but unable to predict how and where these patterns will be. You're going to play with gaps and breaks within the line, between phrases and words, to activate this sensibility and invite your reader to go on a "hike through the woods" with you, whether this hike is real or imagined.

1. Think about a time you were trying to go somewhere, but you were lost. This can be on a hike—maybe you got turned around for a bit, lost your way?—or in a car or in a city or at a beach or on a bike ride... you get the idea! Brainstorm a few examples and then choose the one that tugs at you the most right now, for whatever reason. Which example can you visualize best? Don't think about why. Just jot down where you were, where you tried to go, and/or where you ended up (or didn't).

2. Were you alone during this wandering? Were you with anyone (or any animal)? Make notes.

3. What mood were you in when you began your journey? What mood came over you as you lost yourself?

4. Think back in time to when you had an emotional crisis about something—anything. (This does not have to be related to your wandering experience.) Jot down what this crisis was about.

5. Jot down two colors that come to mind—the first colors that you visualize when reading this step of the prompt.

6. You're ready to begin. Begin the moment you realize you are lost and describe the place with as much detail as you can. Write and write— don't worry about form. Build in who you were with, what you thought you knew, where you thought you were headed, what mood you were in. And then try to connect this moment to the other crisis, the one in part 4. Maybe you could recall it. Maybe you can create an analogy that connects to it. Maybe it can appear through metaphor. Bring in the colors that you named in part 5. You can write through this wandering so that your poem ends when you've found your way. You can write into the space of being lost so that the poem ends without resolution. This is your choice.

7. Once you have a draft, play with spacing—gaps. Add breaths (using the tab key) between words, between sentences. You can do this if your poem is a prose poem. Or you can organize your poem into stanzas of either regular or irregular lengths and then add organic spaces within them. Choose the places to create these gaps by feel, not logic. Later, you can go back and reconsider some of the gaps, but for now, allow yourself the freedom to add light and shade as you wish, expansively.

[Pray]
Leslie Harrison

I test the reality of this slippery day

                    already easing out of reach

I pick minutes for hours

              in the meadow and this does not

                          help me

the clouds the trees   the trees rasp

                like ancient crickets

phlegmy in the way that old things

              are never really loud

look at the horses

        look

           at their four fragile knees

kneel later

     kneel

       kneel when they've given you a box

a closet built of dirt   its weighty

                    stone   handle

then you can kneel then you can pray

                        pray for the rest of your life

        kneeling

                    for years

as the meadow appears

                    and falls under snow   pray with a voice

full of dried leaves full   of falling water

                            voice of new

                                growth new snow

pray

        pray as hard as you can   to the horses

                            skittering

                                startled

                                    away

Cinematic, Moving Image
Placing our Past

What does it mean to animate our past—going to the heart of a story about our life and collecting details about the place and people at that time? You can create an "I" that is also the "eye" of a camera lens panning a scene. This I/eye, like a video camera lens, sweeps through place and time and also collects moving details into your observations.

I keep thinking about Larry Levis's "Elegy Ending in the Sound of a Skipping Rope" (a poem over 300 lines long!) about witnessing political turmoil in Belgrade. The poem begins,

> All I have left of that country is this torn scrap
> Of engraved lunacy, worth less now
>
> Than it was then, for then it was worth nothing,
> Or nothing more than
>
> The dust a wren bathes in,
>
> The fountain dry in the park off the Zeleni Venac,
> The needles of the pines dry above it (1–7).

Consider how you can write about place as though you are both an "I" who was there and also an "eye" that, like a filmmaker's camera lens, focuses on and brings into the emotional story details from a place.

1.   Brainstorm places where you've lived and experienced turmoil of any kind (personal, political, or both). You can think about places long

ago in your past or places in your recent past. You can think about places you've traveled for brief periods or places you've spent many years. Make a list of places, and next to each, jot down memories as well as details of each place. As you do this, you'll find that one place sticks in your mind more than the others. Once you realize this, choose this place to be the focus of your poem.

2. Once you've chosen the place to focus on, jot down sensory details you remember, names of the people who were there, things you've said or you heard, and/or questions you had about yourself, that place, or the world as it was at that time. Brainstorm one object from that time that you remember.

3. You're ready to begin your poem. Begin by describing the object from that place and use it as a diving board to leap into the waters of the place you have decided to focus on. Include the details from your brainstorm, including the people who were there. As you write, linger in your descriptions of objects (things or plants). Ask yourself what else you can say—and what this object means to the larger mood of the poem. Think, too, about who your poem animates; you're welcome to invite glimpses of dialogue into your poem. Allow, too, the "I" to express thoughts about the process of recalling this place and time in your life: "I once thought…" "I asked myself…" "I wondered…" "I wished I could" are phrases you can fold into your poem.

4. As you find yourself nearing the end of your poem, think back to the beginning and try to redescribe the object that started your exploration. What does this object mean to you—and to the place? Can you describe it using metaphors? How do you feel about it now, and how does the way you describe this object express a feeling you have about it or about the place itself (or both)?

5. Aim for longer lines (five beats or longer) if you can. You might find it helpful to break the poem into sections, either numbered or un-numbered. Aim for a longer poem—fifty lines or more—if you can.

The Hearing, Sarajevo

Heathen

I once believed you caught a bird in your hands
                     as if what was happening in me was love.

It was a photograph, a red cardinal cradled in your palms
and I believed it so fully,   the moment of believing it,   a gasp,

intake of breath,   the way I'm willing to believe
everything unaccountable.   You told me it was stunned

against the window is all,   and you'd gone and picked it up,
not caught it,   but three years later I still believed

it flew into your hands,   as easily as I did,   or tried to do
stunning myself like that,   and you refused to pick me up.

I'm waiting at the bus stop in Sarajevo,   still believing.

Sparrows flutter around my feet so close I can make out each
individual feather   hewed to the breast

like the ninety-nine names of God
                     written on the dome of the mosque.

Won't you hold one small beast
of me in your palm   not a question?

                     but a prescription. For loving me back?

Ear bent down to the bird of my mouth when I ask.

What does it say about what kind of love it is
                              that I believed you caught a bird mid-

            flight and it settled into the nest of your fingers,

effortless! Both the trick and the belief in it.

                                                                  *

Nameless birds against clouds now
                        behind the stone walls of the madrassa,

in the ancient room where travelers
                        were always welcomed in and given shelter,

find me in the hole in the dirt beneath the flagstones
where the Haggadah was hidden, buried during the wars.

Daisy-cutter bombs, burn bags, hellhounds, so much spectacle

    guest is God   waiting,

                                                                  *

I once loved what would outlast pain
                        but you are like these birds who come and go
in my dreams;
                        with whom I have no language to share.

The adhan is calling now,
his voice telling a story that never ends.

I hope you can hear me from here.

The Ghost of the Present

Brainstorm a list of places that you have felt especially alive, afraid, happy, sad, angry, or joyful. Choose one that connects with you the most right now, and jot down a list of descriptions of this place. Include colors, scents/foods, plants, animals, and materials (stone, wood, etc.). Now, do a bit of research into the history of this place. What story does this place carry with it? This can be family lore or town history, in the recent past or distant past. Jot down notes about the information (as well as where you found it, in case you need it someday).

Begin a poem addressed to the place itself, in the second person ("you") or by describing a person in this place in the third person ("he," "she," "they," or by name), and incorporate your notes as well as the history that you learned. Try to include one question. Try to repeat one word or phrase of your choice three times. (If a ghost appears in your poem, welcome them in.)

Aim for a poem longer than fourteen lines.

Trying to Name What Doesn't Change

Naomi Shihab Nye

Roselva says the only thing that doesn't change
is train tracks. She's sure of it.
The train changes, or the weeds that grow up spidery
by the side, but not the tracks.
I've watched one for three years, she says,
and it doesn't curve, doesn't break, doesn't grow.

Peter isn't sure. He saw an abandoned track
near Sabinas, Mexico, and says a track without a train
is a changed track. The metal wasn't shiny anymore.
The wood was split and some of the ties were gone.

Every Tuesday on Morales Street
butchers crack the necks of a hundred hens.
The widow in the tilted house
spices her soup with cinnamon.
Ask her what doesn't change.

Stars explode.
The rose curls up as if there is fire in the petals.
The cat who knew me is buried under the bush.

The train whistle still wails its ancient sound
but when it goes away, shrinking back
from the walls of the brain,
it takes something different with it every time.

Celebrity

The Beatles documentary, *Get Back,* makes me think a lot about celebrities and what it means to feel immersed in the life of another artist. I also think about this in relationship to Taylor Swift. What *is* fandom? What is the nature of that yearning—friendship, creativity, collaboration, desire, a mix of all of these things? I've been a fan of many different artists over the years. Actors. Musicians. Writers. Visual artists. One of my best friends in high school was a Prince superfan, and her extreme knowledge and love of him rubbed off on me—and because of her passion for his music, I know so many of his albums, B-sides, and life details. I'm fascinated by how fandom *can* rub off on someone else—the magic taking over, becoming something new. In this way, the celebrity is a person and *also* someone else because of the magic in what they have made. What they have done.

How might a poem, as a vessel, become a transformative act that allows us to unpack what it means to love what someone makes so much that you think you love them (whatever that means to you)?

Poems are acts of magic: we wish, we dream, we raise the dead, we create a new reality. What power can you harness by connecting the medium—and I mean "medium" in all of its registers, including corresponding with the dead—of language to uncover what *your* fandom means, what your relationship to someone else's art can say about love, fear, joy, desire, grief, or what it means to be alive?

Some poets imagine themselves to speak with a celebrity or imagine a celebrity in certain situations. For instance, the poems of Amorak Huey and W. Todd Kaneko in *Slash / Slash* explore Slash and Axl Rose's dynamic, tension, feud, and friendship in the band Guns N' Roses and also mix in the character Mr. Spock from *Star Trek*. For this prompt, you're welcome to imagine yourself in conversation with a celebrity or writing about the time you met or had an encounter with a celebrity.

1. Freewrite about bands you love and the musicians in them, artists you love, and actors that you love (and particular movies or TV shows they've been in). You can include comedians, other kinds of performers, and writers as well. Make a list; jot down details that come to mind about what you love and why (such as your first time hearing a song, a particular role that captivated you, etc.).

2. Have you ever encountered a celebrity? By going to a show and meeting them backstage? Have you ever run into a celebrity randomly somewhere unexpected? Jot down details if this pertains to you!

3. Now, think about a secret that you have inside of you, big or small: something you've done, something you feel, something you said or wished you said. Imagine yourself telling one of the celebrities on your list this secret. Who would it be and why?

4. *Option 1:* If you've chosen the celebrity that you've met to tell your secret to, begin a poem about this meeting: where you were, what the celebrity looked like, what you said, what you did not say. Repeat the lines "I wanted" three times, and each time try to outdo yourself by writing about a want that is a little more outlandish than the last. As your poem concludes, you can choose to tell the celebrity the secret or you can allude to it while keeping it hidden.

5. *Option 2:* If you've chosen a celebrity that you really admire and have never met, imagine places that you could encounter them in your life: café, grocery store, hiking trail, McDonald's, bank parking lot, a room in your living space, etc. Begin by describing the celebrity's expression and then the room/place where you're imagining yourself. Allude to why they are there (imagine a reason other than that you invited them to be there). Include details about where you are and then imagine that you are about to tell them your secret. What do you say? What do you not say?

Suggestion: After you have a draft, try your poem in couplets or quatrains!

Slash and Mr. Spock Sitting in the Waffle House at the End of the Universe

W. Todd Kaneko & Amorak Huey

In the dying light of the final star,
there will be breakfast at that last
truck stop between here and oblivion,

a pair of quasars sunny side up,
a bundle of flimsy bacon and a bottle
of Jack Daniels. Spock can't help
but admire that hue and ooze
of yolk, that way an egg is all

things—an embryo, a planet, a goop
of sunshine with a prehistoric bob
and quiver for the fork. Outside,
the truckers shake their heads
at the loads that won't ever reach

their destinations: dilithium crystals
burned out for warp drives, wall clocks
with hands stuck forever at ten and two,
cans of chili con carne and cling peaches,

their expiration dates now irrelevant.
The Vulcan takes a slug of whiskey
as he observes Slash preparing to eat
a waffle, pouring syrup into every crevice
without spilling any onto the plate.

Just eat it, Spock says. *At any moment*
we could tumble ass over ashes, collapse
back into that cosmic dust that spawned
us in the vacuum. Slash takes a first bite
and wipes a dribble of syrup from his chin
on his sleeve. *That's rock and roll*, he says
with his mouth full. Spock cannot argue logic
for the supernova, reason for catastrophe,
appetite for the eater of worlds.

Patterning Shadow & Light

Sometimes, stanzas tumble away from the left margin, creating almost leaf-shapes on the page that cascade down it in a pseudo-pattern. The effect of reading poems like this is of stepping in and out of leaf patterns. The maple leaves are all the same shape, but clustered on a branch, they create similar yet different shadows on the sidewalk.

This prompt engages with this strategy—what I'm thinking of as a patterning of shadow and light—where lines indent away from the left margin in slightly irregular patterns *in a poem with regular stanzas.* So you're creating shadows with the same kind of object—the same kind of leaf (or stanza). I've noticed so many poets experimenting with this approach to form, and I invite you to think about Cheswayo Mphanza's "Paean to Chikumbi" as a beautiful example. It begins,

> And the village was steeped
>   in red clay soil. Stars whistling
>   across sky. Drywood
>
>   termites flying
> over us every spring.
>   We thought we
>
>   could pluck some if we extended
> our little arms, barely
>   hopping off the ground (1–9).

You're welcome to think about gaps and distances so that the effect of the poem you write is that of stepping in and out of shadows.

1. Think about places that are sacred to you. This can be a home, a place you've traveled, a place you've visited, a placed you've dreamed about. How are you defining sacred? What does this word mean to you? And how do you associate it with place? Jot down a few sentences that come to mind (where you ruminate on these questions and also connect your ideas to specific places).

2. What does the sky or ceiling look like in the sacred place that is connecting with you the most right now? Describe it as best you can. What song or sound do you associate with this space? Jot it down.

3. What hurt or wound did you bring to this space? (Or perhaps, what hurt or wound did this space give you?) Jot this down.

4. Begin your poem by folding in your details from steps 1–3. You might want to begin with step three or you might want to begin with step one or two. You choose! Try to organize your poem into stanzas of regular length (tercets, quatrains, cinquains—your choice). Once you've done this, think about the mood you want to create with your poem. Is it one of cascading movement? Is it more severe or startling? Then pattern your line indentations accordingly so that the visual effect connects with the mood you want to evoke.

Paean to Chikumbi

Cheswayo Mphanza

And the village was steeped
    in red clay soil. Stars whistling
        across sky. Drywood

    termites flying
over us every spring.
        We thought we

    could pluck some if we extended
our little arms, barely
        hopping off the ground.

    Cousins' small greased
        hands sliding down
            grandma's legs, swollen

        with arthritis.
Attempting to force
    the pain into light

tremors. Aunts in
    bold chitenges—
infants strapped to their

        backs, pounding
corn bende na munsi.
        White corn powder

    later turned to nshima.
Songs falling from
        their mouths. My ears

to the ground, picking up
Bemba lyrics:

      Ubunga bwa male lito
bwasalangana lito tabumona
          beni lito ale kanshinguluke

ale kanshinguluke kanshinguluke
    ka lito ale kambweluluke
    ale kambweluluke

kambweluluke ka lito.

    My nose to the sky, inhaling
        today's hand-washed
laundry hanging on copper

              wires between mango
trees. Frothy soap tablets
         in buckets of water
     serving as detergent.
           Scents of mustard greens,
kandolo, impwa. Papaya tree

     that blossomed one fruit.
We chopped it down.
   So sweet, we ate the seeds.

Fertilizer we placed in
         cornfields. Our skin developing
rashes for the harvest.

          Once they bloomed.
     we husked corn silk
        and placed them on

our heads, pretending to be
        bazungu. Sugar cane stalk
we snapped and peeled

                        with our teeth. Sometimes
busting our lips. Tasting blood
        in the sweet

                        mulch. Maybe dreaming
                of sugar water and a taste
                                of chitumbuas.

        Sand hills where honey
bees formed hives.
Our hands reaching

                for combs, numbed to the
stinging pain in the name
                of sweetness.

                        Tongues licking fresh
                honey off each comb piece
before we passed it

        to the next. Blind snakes
                        grandpa caught
by hand. Severing

                        heads before wrapping
                their bodies in banana leaves
                and burning them.

Small sacrifice
        or ritual to keep us
                alive. Listening

to his omens that forbade
            us from pointing at graves.
When my voice

        became too rough to him,
                        the walk he made me take
        to the mulberry tree.

                        Branch
                    he ordered I snap off myself.
                    Its body covered

        in ripe berries. His swing
                of the luscious blows
                            against my back,

                    staining my good
            shirt tie-dyed with
                        berry juice. Crowngrass

                where we preyed
on grasshoppers before
    we roasted them on

        woodfire.
                    Guava trees I climbed
to glance at chameleons

        nesting. Their changing colors—
chartreuse, tuscany, emerald,
        and lime—

            signaling ripeness.
                        Sometimes malice:
the seasonal floods.

Soiled streams running
with kapentas.
                    We caught kapentas

                                        in streams by hand.
            Our oversized shirts
                        serving as nets.
        We squatted and cast
            our shirts in the muddy
streams to taste some

                            form of nyama. Seasoned
                them with the onions
        from grandma's wild garden.

Saving some to rub on our
        bodies, waiting for hair
            to bloom.

                                        Ancient myths
                            we believed. Shock that sent
                me back to the burning

        woodstove. My fall in
                the tin tub
filled with boiling water.

                Sores and blisters
                            peeling skin off.
                                Water's

        heat peeled like a map
                from my back like
        the kapenta's skeleton.

Energizing the Object from the Tale

Brainstorm objects from religious stories, myths, legends, and fairy tales. You're welcome to refresh your memory of a tale that comes to you by rereading it or skimming a summary. Choose the object that sticks in your mind the most right now, for whatever reason.

Brainstorm some narrative details from the story that would be part of this object's life. What does this object look like? Feel like?

Write a poem where you imagine a scene where you and another person are encountering this object today, out of context, and disagreeing about what this object means, does, or could do. You are welcome to use dialogue! Try to describe one detail of this object in three different ways in your poem, using similes or metaphors.

Ode to Pomegranates

Aimee Seu

Garnet jackpot packed tight
in this diction of foam.
Magenta honeycomb
of sluice & syrup.
I hold you up to the sun
& you glow. You are an edible jewel.
Renegade red & ambrosian as swearing.
The first person to want
to put their mouth there
on a woman must have been
the first person. Frill of rind,
then alien brain. Pleasure *should* be messy.
Years ago, a girl licked my blood
off her fingers. Years ago, I licked
a boy's bloody nose off his face.
And now you, palm-sized bomb
of stickiness, remind me.
This geode to crack open & plunder.
You make me want to wear a corset
just to cut myself free.
You make me want to wear a dress
to hike up my skirt & run
barefoot through the equinox.
You are a fireside tongue-kiss. Queen
of all raspberries & coagulating magma.
The Romanov daughters' bodices
were sewn with so many cursed diamonds
they deflected assassins' bullets.
So they were bayoneted on the floor.
If obsession were color. If rubies
could melt. Lying here in the yard

with my kitchen knife & stained nails
the prince of darkness couldn't take me
alive. Watch me eat the fruit
of the underworld & remain here
uncaptured. You are a smuggled prize.
Sweet slant rhyme of nourish
& perish, I slice & thumb open
a giant's heavy heart.
I drink the blood of immortals.
The knowledge of good bores me
but oh, the sugary knowledge of evil.
Oh, to have the scent of a lover
on your hands all day, to be tarnished
by scarlet oblivion. I want to lie in bed
with you with the window open
cradling you, consuming you
ravenously, picking you apart
as the morning rain begins
to scatter itself. As long as I live I want
to taste every last capsuled drop.

Spinning a Yarn, Unspooling Logic
Prose Poem

This exercise invites you to write into feeling, into energy, into the emotional core of an experience.

Write a prose poem as if it were a set of instructions, a "how to," yet these instructions can break into story, into song, into memory, into history. In other words, the poem will begin with a direction or even two, but you can undo this and write into the imagery, mood, and/or memories that come up for you.

1. Begin by making a list of people or kinds of people who have given you advice (wanted, unwanted, helpful, unhelpful). Which person brings up the most feelings for you? Choose this person and their advice as the jumping off point for your poem.

2. Jot down three colors and two animals, insects, or reptiles.

3. Set a timer for twenty minutes and be prepared to write without stopping.

4. Begin your poem with the piece of advice you've been given, and write everything that comes into your mind without stopping for twenty minutes. Try to write about a set of instructions, and then break these instructions apart. How can the instructions fail? How can they become mythic, larger than life?

As you write, try to incorporate colors and animals, insects, or reptiles.

Even if something comes up that surprises you, even if you think nothing comes up, write all of your thoughts down without stopping. (You can write "I am at a blank because…" into your poem, for example, and push past it.)

When you are finished, reread your prose poem and add one more sentence (or two) that you think could be missing.

How to Dismantle a Heart

Rodney Gomez

My mother used to say the heart makes music, but I've never found the keys.
Maybe it's the way I was brought into the world: dragged across a river in the
night's quiet breathing, trampling through trash and tired runaways as if
tearing a window's curtains. We were barred from entry but repeatedly
returned, each time becoming a darker part of a tunnel or a truck bed. The sky
was so still the stars flickered like carbide lamps. We told time through the
landmarks of the dead like cataphiles—the warren of a little girl's murder, the
wolf's irrigation pipe. When you see enough unwinding, beating is replaced by
the safety of wings. This isn't goodness. The voiceless are never neutral. Bones
sway to elegy. Ebony burrows into the earth as a refugee. I grew up, eventually,
but the sun was like a cliff with a false bottom: you'd drop and come out the
top again. Enough carcasses draped over the dry brush. Enough water towers
empty as busted rattles. When you're a child, the heart has a stiff neck and
demands to be played. Later, it limps. Before my knees could begin to ache, I
crawled to the levee looking for a broken string. Some wayward zil. I stretched
my heart over a manhole and drummed it with broken pliers. It wouldn't even
quaver. It snapped back into a seed, dry and shriveled and blank.

Mythic Self, Mythic Story

This prompt invites you to think about the ways a mythical figure can unlock personal memories. I keep thinking about the end of Adrienne Rich's poem "Diving into the Wreck," where a sea diver excavates the wreckage of the past with "a book of myths / in which / our names do not appear."

How might a myth invite you to travel—both away from and yet closer to, perhaps even in the same poem!—an event in your life? How might myth also invite you to think about the ways stories do or do not include us in their telling—stories about history, about place, about literature? What would you do to wrestle with these stories in which you might be absent and how would you include yourself there? What would your retelling look like?

1. Brainstorm myths that interest you, speak to you, tug at you, or even bother you. (You're welcome to refresh your memory with some googling!) You're welcome to define "myth" broadly, as in Rich's poem, as a place where something happened and our stories about it are not complete.

2. Choose a myth from your list to focus on in your poem. Jot down three scents that a character in this myth might have smelled. Jot down four colors. Jot down one sound. Write down the most troubling thing one of the mythical people or animals had to deal with in the story.

3. Now, think about why you chose this myth. How does it connect with you personally? Does it make you think of any memories from your own life? How so and why? Jot down details!

4. You are ready to begin your poem. Start with as clear a description from the myth as you can, drawing from the scents, colors, and the sound that you brainstormed. Try to include three similes in your poem (you can draw from the colors and scents to help you!) Allow your mind to meander, to continue to imagine this scene, and as you do, begin to shift into describing your own memory, your own life. What conflict emerges? What questions? What emotions? Allow all of this into your poem. Is your myth a larger metaphor for a feeling? Can you build this metaphor into your poem? You can try playing with sentence fragments as your poem deepens into your own memory. Ask yourself what it means to you to include yourself in the myth you chose.

Aim for 16–50 lines *or* write a prose poem, which is a poem without line breaks.

from Episode 1: Labyrinth

Oliver de la Paz

The boy hears the beast. The pad of the beast's hooves, quiet vowels sung to a sleeper. The boy listens to keep himself awake. He thinks of spiders on the edges of their webs, the ballet they dance on their self-made filigree. He thinks of an azalea sewn into the hem of a dress. The boy thinks, *this kind of thinking led me to the labyrinth.* Its black geodes. Its promises of wild crystal blooms held within. Morning digresses into night, and the beast's song laces its orbit through limestone causeways. It grows smaller and smaller until imperceptible. The boy soon misses the song. The beast's idle stroll. The faint breeze to remind that there is anything there in the widening dark.

The Red Wheel—

I'm titling this prompt "The Red Wheel—" because I've been thinking a lot about William Carlos Williams's famous (and sometimes frustrating) poem "The Red Wheelbarrow." There is so much to say about this tiny poem. You've likely encountered Williams's Modernist, image-driven poem in a survey class, or perhaps you've encountered it in an anthology. Perhaps you've taught it to a group of puzzled students. Maybe you've been a puzzled student reading this poem at one point. Maybe you've always loved this poem for its instantaneously vivid, fresh imagery. I have.

For me, the word "glazed" makes the whole poem pivot into a new mood. The poem sets this up with the musicality of "glazed" and "rain" (those "a" sounds) and also the cold beauty that the word "glazed" invites us to think about. Like a cake in a bakery window. Ornamental, precious, beautifully decorous—and yet. The red wheelbarrow that the poem offers us, made beautiful and still through the rainwater, is not being put to work. The object has been transformed from its intended use, for a time. Within the poem's stillness.

Maybe, for you, the poem is about labor—the work that the wheelbarrow must do for the farm. Maybe it's a poem purely about color—red and white—and visual effects. Maybe for you there's a whole backstory to the poem informed by the speaker-poet, Williams, who was a doctor and made house calls. Perhaps to a sick patient at a farm? (Actually, the poem was supposedly inspired by a fisherman that Williams met who kept chickens.) Maybe the rainwater invokes sadness. Maybe the white chickens invoke a higher being—doves. Peace. Hope. Maybe the chickens are just chickens.

We could close read this poem endlessly, couldn't we? *But what are you getting at here?* you might be thinking.

I'm thinking about Williams's "The Red Wheel Barrow" because I've been considering the way that poems that zero in on objects and mini scenes can carry emotional weight in a manuscript or sequence. I keep coming back to Williams's famous statement, "No ideas but in things." What might the effect be of a shorter, image-driven poem—a poem focusing on describing a thing or scene but without offering a backstory—within a manuscript? How might a poem like this pack a punch when in conversation with other poems you've written? What does it mean for you, right now, to intensely describe an object or scene without offering any characters, any specific emotions—even an "I?"

A poem like "The Red Wheelbarrow" in a manuscript or sequence—or in conversation with a handful of other poems—functions like a wheel. A tiny poem that isn't directly "about" the thing your other poems more directly focus on can *roll* the larger project forward all the same. The imagery creates energy in itself. "No ideas but in things."

This prompt has two paths forward.

First option (or path):

1. If you are working on a book, look through your manuscript and notice objects you've written about in other poems. Jot down two or three.

2. Think about your objects. Imagine each one in a setting: in relationship to a place and perhaps other objects or animals. Which object strikes you the most, now, for whatever reason? Choose this one as the focus of your poem.

3. Describe the object in its scene using colors (two or three) and details of what is around it. Look back and trim your poem so it focuses as closely on its descriptions as possible. Choose short lines. As you whittle your poem down, think about one part of the description that creates energy in the poem (like "glazed" in "The Red Wheelbarrow").

Tip: When you position your poem in a manuscript, don't put it directly next to the poem with the object it's in conversation with.

Poetry Studio

Second option (or path):

1. Brainstorm scenes from childhood where you were alone and observing something (a room, a yard, a car, a forest, a city, a beach, etc.). Jot down what comes to you and think carefully about the objects in the scenes that you're recalling.

2. Choose one scene to focus on—the scene that comes to you now the most vividly—and describe it as clearly and concisely as you can. Include colors, textures, and the objects around it. Look back and trim your poem so it focuses as closely on its descriptions as possible. Choose short lines. As you whittle your poem down, think about one part of the description that creates energy in the poem (like "glazed" in "The Red Wheelbarrow").

When you are finished, you might ask yourself, *Is my poem enough of a poem?* Rest assured, the answer is yes.

The Red Wheelbarrow

William Carlos Williams

so much depends
upon

a red wheel
barrow

glazed with rain
water

beside the white
chickens

And Scene!

I watched a movie recently that I thought was going to do one thing, and then it become so awesomely invested in its genre—dark comedy—that it was just electrifying! It was so over the top that I simply admired how the premise became more and more exaggerated. The dark humor more and more cutting. It did not do the thing I thought it would do at all.

No, I'm not going to tell you what movie it is. And the reason *isn't* that I'm protecting you from a plot spoiler. (Though I would *always* protect you from a plot spoiler.) Anyway, what's the real reason I'm not telling you which movie I'm thinking about? Because I want you to imagine you're filming a moment of your life as a scene in your poem. This prompt moves away from an external source and into your memories.

You won't be writing about a specific movie. I'm inviting you to write about a moment of your own life as though you're filming a scene. In doing so, I want you to free yourself from autobiography a bit. You can become mythic. You can bend the rules of place and time. You can react to this past self you're encountering as though they're a character separate from you. Your poem can skid around corners and practically catch fire.

For this prompt, once you commit to an emotion or mood, dig in. And then dig deeper. Let similes and metaphors work for you; try to load your poem with as many of them as possible.

1. Think about a time in your life when you felt *so* yourself but now can't quite imagine doing what you once did. Where were you? What were you doing? Jot down some places and words to jog your memory.

2. Go to Walmart or Target online, browse what's on sale or what's being marketed to you right now, and write down two or three objects (and describe them in detail).

3. Now look at your list of experiences from step one. Which are you chuckling over or raising your eyebrows about now, for *whatever reason*? This will be the scene of your poem.

4. Before you begin, jot down one body part (or name of a bone or muscle), one piece of technology from any era, and one object or toy from your youth.

5. Now you're ready to begin! Start your poem in the scene, and as you describe it and write about the past self that is there, build in as many similes and metaphors as you can from step four. Fold the items from step two into your poem so that they become metaphors ("couch of longing"). Try to make your poem as vivid as possible; once you've landed on your poem's mood, *dig in*.

Tip: Try your poem in a single stanza!

Poetry Studio

Heaven and Its Static

Mary Biddinger

When I drink amaretto sours I get my old self back
and it's pretty awful. There's a reason we left her
at the bottom of the mountain with a faux soldier.
She's probably still preaching various weak beliefs.
Or wearing that sweater with the metal brackets.
It's amazing we traversed the entire valley on foot
but we were younger and didn't think about feet.
When the wrought iron café chair left waffles all
up and down my ass, I laughed it off, got hungry.
While she was feeling her way out of catacombs
I auditioned a few prospective masseuses. Shame
we had to separate on account of passport drama.
My new incarnation fixed problems preemptively.
Threw out the Dutch baby before its edges burned.
Remained on a couch when the DJ played ABBA.
But then, inevitably, there's a mirrored bathroom
corridor and a stall with a stranger on the phone,
only the call is for me. She puts it on speaker so
even my frenemies can hear the intimate static.
Soap flows directly from dispenser to tile floor.

Begin Again

Every May, I think of Philip Larkin's "The Trees," a meditation on what it means to live within life's cycles, to face new growth in the aftermath of the past. I lose myself in the way the envelope rhymes fold up each quatrain every time I read it. But the part I'm thinking about is the poem's final four words: *Begin afresh, afresh, afresh.*

This prompt is about energizing a poem to create and recreate itself on the page.

1. Think about something you saw very recently—something you wish you didn't see. This could be a TV show, something on the news, something in your neighborhood, something in your yard. By "recently" I'm thinking within the past six months, though if you can write about something very recent, the better.

2. What was it that you wished you didn't see? And why? Jot down all of this with as much detail as possible.

3. Jot down two scents—one from the scene and one (any scent) not from the scene.

4. Go to a book on your shelf, open a random page, and jot down the first two words that catch your eye.

5. Draft a poem where you try to begin describing the thing you witnessed and attempt to begin describing it again in your poem at least twice. You can use repetition to guide you. For example, *Yesterday, I watched.... Yesterday, I watched....*

As you write your poem, describe the thing you witnessed in as much detail as possible, using shorter lines. Incorporate the scents and words from your brainstorm. What is it that you *wished* happened? Can you let this into your poem?

The month after the cruelest month

Anne Barngrover

is silk and velvet, redbuds and forsythia,
lace-white pear trees backlit

in a streetlamp's planetary glow.
A grinning dog chases cars in tall grass's

gold tassels, and some fool
burns wet green wood in the near

distance, the rising smoke in the trees
with a bad smell that creates no heat,

no clear purpose. How I no longer feel
out-of-love but simply *not-loving.*

I established this pattern years ago.
For one month I believe

I'm someone's dream girl. I fall
for someone's charm like a migrating bird—

the bright flicker of feathers, the rare
trill threading the dogwoods—then gone.

I'm down on my luck again, pissing off
every man around. I'm no one's

dream; therefore I am everyone's
foe. Call me *jaded*—it fits

me like a dress that's so tight
I can't properly sit down. Every woman

must come to a crossroads. Oh, charmer,
I have learned your bright alphabet

of night-blooming flowers.
There will always be dirt in your nails

and smoke on your breath.
There will always be smoke in the trees.

Long Lines and the Traveling "I"

Imagine you are viewing a landscape you are familiar with from a birds-eye view, as though you're in a hot air balloon or in a helicopter or airplane. What do you see? What do you hear? What do you notice as you travel over it? Now imagine that you landed and have your feet on the ground in a particular place in the landscape. What do you see? Hear? Smell? Taste? Who is there? Who is not there? Write an expansive poem of long lines—we're channeling Walt Whitman here!—that is at least twenty-five lines long. As a jumping off point, you can temporarily title it "Song of _____," after "Song of Myself."

from "Song of Myself" (1892 version)

Walt Whitman

1

I celebrate myself, and sing myself,
And what I assume you shall assume,
For every atom belonging to me as good belongs to you.

I loafe and invite my soul,
I lean and loafe at my ease observing a spear of summer grass.

My tongue, every atom of my blood, form'd from this soil, this air,
Born here of parents born here from parents the same, and their parents the same,
I, now thirty-seven years old in perfect health begin,
Hoping to cease not till death.

Creeds and schools in abeyance,
Retiring back a while sufficed at what they are, but never forgotten,
I harbor for good or bad, I permit to speak at every hazard,
Nature without check with original energy.

2

Houses and rooms are full of perfumes, the shelves are crowded with perfumes,
I breathe the fragrance myself and know it and like it,
The distillation would intoxicate me also, but I shall not let it.

The atmosphere is not a perfume, it has no taste of the distillation, it is odorless,
It is for my mouth forever, I am in love with it,
I will go to the bank by the wood and become undisguised and naked,
I am mad for it to be in contact with me.

The smoke of my own breath,
Echoes, ripples, buzz'd whispers, love-root, silk-thread, crotch and vine,
My respiration and inspiration, the beating of my heart, the passing of blood and
     air through my lungs,

The sniff of green leaves and dry leaves, and of the shore and dark-color'd sea-
    rocks, and of hay in the barn,
The sound of the belch'd words of my voice loos'd to the eddies of the wind,
A few light kisses, a few embraces, a reaching around of arms,
The play of shine and shade on the trees as the supple boughs wag,
The delight alone or in the rush of the streets, or along the fields and hill-sides,
The feeling of health, the full-noon trill, the song of me rising from bed and
    meeting the sun.

Have you reckon'd a thousand acres much? have you reckon'd the earth much?
Have you practis'd so long to learn to read?
Have you felt so proud to get at the meaning of poems?

Stop this day and night with me and you shall possess the origin of all poems,
You shall possess the good of the earth and sun, (there are millions of suns left,)
You shall no longer take things at second or third hand, nor look through the
    eyes of the dead, nor feed on the spectres in books,
You shall not look through my eyes either, nor take things from me,
You shall listen to all sides and filter them from your self.

Companion Poem to Long Lines and the Traveling "I"

This poem will be an extension of your last poem; you can think of this as "Part II," where you'll merge this poem with the previous draft eventually. Or, you can think of this as a separate poem in conversation with your first "Long Lines and the Traveling 'I'" poem. I want you to go through the same meditation as you did in the previous poem but choose a slightly different location or region OR choose the same location or region but choose distinctly different details to zero in on.

Creative Revision

Revision Prompt—Shuffle Forward, Shuffle Back

Sometimes, when I'm stuck while revising a poem, I realize that the poem's real energy comes about four lines in. Letting go can be hard to do, but a trim—or shuffling forward in your poem—can do amazing things for the poem's energy *and* how you situate the reader. This prompt is in two steps:

1. Look for a place within your poem between two to four lines into it (perhaps even five lines in!) where there is a radical shift in energy. Does the pace quicken? Does the tone change? Start the poem there, and take the original beginning and place it after your new beginning. To ensure the poem makes sense, you may need to add an additional word or phrase, but you might not. (I've found this often isn't needed!)

2. Now look at your ending. Look two to three lines above where you end the poem, and end it there. Shuffle the original ending up before your new ending, perhaps right before it, perhaps much earlier in the poem.

Revision Prompt—Heart Opener

With "heart opener," I am borrowing from yoga terminology a bit. I'm thinking of a stretch that opens the back and shoulders to release tension in the ribs and chest area. If you're into thinking about chakras, or energy centers in the body, you can think about this exercise as opening up a heart chakra: your *poem*'s heart chakra. Where can our language find joy even in a poem about sorrow? How can you activate the language at the heart of your poem?

1. Print the poem you've chosen to work on, and read it out loud. Midway through it or toward the end, search for a place where you feel very satisfied with how the language is communicating what you feel it needs to for your poem. Find an excerpt where you feel like you can pat yourself on the back and say, *Good job! I love this image.* Underline this.

2. Aha! Now, this is the part of the poem you're going to open up— gently, even just a little bit. The more satisfied you are with the part of the poem you're working on, the better for this exercise. If you're having complicated feelings about this, let them in.

3. Now that you've found the spot for your heart opener, take a piece of paper and pen out, and rewrite the passage by injecting it with color, repetition, a question, a scent, or a mixture of all of these things. If you find your mind wandering and offering another brief vignette, allow this wandering.

4. When you have your new material, ask yourself what you'd like to take from it and add to your poem. You are opening your poem up and letting new language add to the energy of the spot that you feel is important to the poem's arc.

Your heart opener might invite you to adjust the poem's form (stanza length, line length), and that is perfectly OK! You might prefer the new form, or the new form might invite you to find moments of the poem that you can either trim or expand.

Revision Prompt—Zeroing in on Motif

This prompt will require you to circle back to specific words, phrases, and/or motifs in a draft.

1. Take a look at the draft you chose. What image or description begins the poem? Circle it.

2. Now look for other parts of the poem that already engage this image or description in another way—with synonyms perhaps, or similar objects. Jot these words down.

3. Locate a point midway into your poem where you can build in one of the above words. Revise this section so you are including at least one of them. (One might very well be enough!)

4. Look at the ending. Tweak it so that you are including one of the words from your list somehow (or perhaps another one that comes to mind during this process).

Tip: This prompt can seem deceptively easy, but don't underestimate it! Sometimes a poem that doesn't quite feel finished needs an ending that reflects its beginning. Sometimes, the ending and beginning speak to each other, but in the middle, the reader feels lost at sea.

Revision Prompt—So Long, Object, Hello, Form

When Elizabeth Bishop wrote "One Art," revising draft upon draft, an object that jumpstarted her first version of the poem—losing a pair of reading glasses—ended up being what she cut from a later revision. Sometimes, even though this is hard to do, we need to let go of the obvious thing that led us to start the poem so the poem can grow into something greater than our original impulse. (I encourage you to google Bishop's poem!)

This prompt is in two parts. The first part asks you to take out the original object—the detail, thing, idea, or phrase—that inspired you to write the draft in front of you. The second part invites you to change the poem's form.

But first, this exploration works best if you can apply the activity to a draft where you remember the idea—big or small—behind the poem *and* you've included this object in the poem. (In a sense, you're searching for the "reading-glasses" moment that kicked off the idea and locating it in your draft.) What in this poem have you refused to let go of?

Here is the prompt:

1. Read your draft and look for the object (detail, thing, idea, or phrase)—most likely toward the beginning—that in an obvious way pushed you to write the poem. Cross out this object, even though this might go against your instincts for the poem, and instead replace it with something else. You may include between one to three new images, metaphors, or objects (or a mixture of these things). Your

addition might change the form of your poem, and that is OK. At this point in the prompt, you should feel free to write as much (or as little) as you need to in order to let go of the "reading glasses" that started your poem.

2. Now that you've reconceived the beginning of your poem, notice the form and change it in some way. For example, was your poem in three-line stanzas? Then try couplets, and in creating the couplets, ask yourself, *What do I need to cut or add?* Or, you could try your poem in quatrains if the poem doesn't have stanzas at all, and ask yourself, *How can I adjust the line lengths or line breaks so that I can transform this poem into four-line stanzas (quatrains?).* Slight adjustments in form can invite some very big transformations. Allow any changes that arise as you adjust the form into this revision of your poem.

Tip: I encourage you to open up a new notebook page and imagine yourself freewriting as you revise your poem, creating a new landscape for yourself where you can let in new ideas. Then type out what you've handwritten. You may find that in typing out your draft, you discover important adjustments to the form.

Revision Prompt—"Ready, Set, Action"

This exercise invites you to think about how actions can energize a poem. Imagine a TV set where actors wait for the cameras to roll. *Ready, set, action!* And the clapperboard shuts. Now, everyone is in the middle of doing specific things. If someone is drinking coffee, they are holding a mug a certain way and lifting it to their lips.

1. Print the poem you've chosen to work on. Go through it and circle all of the verbs (action words!). Don't forget about passive voice verbs and "to be" verbs like "is," "am," and "are."

2. Now, comb through your poem, and ask yourself if there are verbs that aren't doing something as interesting as they could. "Moving," "walking," "sitting"—what else could happen, or what more specific smaller action could you think of? Can you think of visual verbs to inject energy into your poem? You don't have to revise each and every verb, but try to be mindful of what you are choosing to change and why. As you revise a verb, you might have an idea about rephrasing an image: allow your ideas into your process. Even if you only choose to swap out two verbs, this revision will create a completely different level of energy in your poem.

Revision Prompt—The Speaker Revealed

Choose a draft where you aren't quite sure the speaker (the voice of the poem, whether there is an "I" speaking, a "we," or the poem is in third person) is being vulnerable enough. Is this a political poem where the speaker is declaiming the ills of X, Y, or Z, but isn't in the poem sharing what is at stake personally? Is there a part of your poem where you aren't really saying what is at stake? Is the poem using humor to the point that a reader could lose where the self is at risk or in joy?

1. For this poem, underline the moment where you think the most important thing, large or small, is happening.

2. Rewrite this section so that you open it up to include the vulnerability the speaker has or what is truly at stake. Try to engage with color, sound, or taste in this moment.

3. Now, as you add this moment back into the poem, allow yourself to make small changes to other sections so that they can resonate with what you added.

Tip: My tip for this exploration is to allow some time to really think about step one, where you locate the most important thing that happens in the poem. Let the poem reveal this moment to you as you read it to yourself: you might be surprised to find that the moment you decide to work on isn't what you had expected.

Revision Prompt—Expansion or Contraction

This prompt asks you to either creatively expand or radically contract a draft of your choice.

1. Choose one draft of a poem that is either fairly long or fairly short. I am not going to define what I mean by long or short; instead, I'd like you to think about the kinds of poems you write and choose one that is either fairly long for you or fairly short for you.

2. For this poem, either expand or contract your draft, radically, by at least nine lines. If you are contracting, ask yourself what you can condense. What happens to the rest of the poem when you do so? If you are expanding, ask yourself where you can get inside an idea or object and expand it from within, perhaps through description or a change in point of view.

Tip: I encourage you to open up a new page in your notebook and imagine yourself freewriting as you revise your poem so you're freeing yourself from the original draft and creating a landscape where you can let in new ideas. Then type it out. You may find that in typing out your draft, you discover important adjustments to what you include or delete.

Acknowledgments

Enormous thanks to the University of Akron Press—Jon Miller, Mary Biddinger, Amy Freels, Brittany LaPointe, and Thea Ledendecker—for trusting me with this book, for giving it a home, and for your advice at every step along the way. I cannot think of a more special home for this book. I also have enormous gratitude to the poets and presses who agreed to have poems in these pages. I'm also thankful for Arik, Josie, and Claire, and my friends and family who heard me talk endlessly about this book at the kitchen table, over coffee, and on walks. Thank you to my fellow poets for all of the poems being written on café tables, at the boardwalk, on buses, over coffee, and shared on the printed page and over screens. I am grateful to the poets who came before me and the poets in community with me. Thank you to my teachers, who lit the path before me.

I have gratitude for the Writing Institute at Sarah Lawrence College and the Provincetown Fine Arts Work Center's 24PearlStreet, where I first crafted and used some of these exercises. I'm also thankful for the writers who participated in my Poetry15 Substack.

Most of all, I'm grateful to all the poets writing in little bits of time carved out of the day. Thank you for writing. Thank you, poets.

Permissions

Kim Addonizio, "New Year's Day" from *Tell Me*. Copyright © 2000 by Kim Addonizio. Reprinted with the permission of The Permissions Company, LLC on behalf of BOA Editions, Ltd., boaeditions.org.

Lucille Clifton, "memory" from *The Collected Poems of Lucille Clifton, 1965–2010*. Copyright © 1996 by Lucille Clifton. Reprinted with the permission of The Permissions Company, LLC on behalf of BOA Editions, Ltd., boaeditions.org.

Luiza Flynn-Goodlett "I Ask the Garden for Comfort." Originally published in *Waxwing* (Fall 2022). © 2022 by Luiza Flynn-Goodlett. Reprinted with the permission of the author.

Kendra DeColo "Love Letter with Nightguard and Liam Neeson." Originally published in *Ilanot Review* (Fall 2022). © 2022 by Kendra DeColo. Reprinted with the permission of the author.

Trey Moody "The Swing Set." Originally published in *Waxwing* (Spring 2022). © 2022 by Trey Moody. Reprinted with the permission of the author.

"Movement Song" from *The Collected Poems of Audre Lorde* by Audre Lorde. Copyright © 1997 by The Audre Lorde Estate. Used by permission of W. W. Norton & Company, Inc.

"White Dog" from *The Rest of Love* by Carl Phillips. Copyright © 2004 by Carl Phillips. Reprinted by permission of Farrar, Straus and Giroux. All Rights Reserved.

"The Sea." Copyright © 2019 by David Baker, from *SWIFT: NEW AND SELECTED POEMS* by David Baker. Used by permission of W. W. Norton & Company, Inc.

Ilya Kaminsky. "We Lived Happily during the War" from *Deaf Republic*. Originally published in Poetry (May 2009). Copyright © 2009, 2018 by Ilya Kaminsky. Reprinted with the permission of The Permissions Company, LLC on behalf of Graywolf Press, Minneapolis, Minnesota, graywolfpress.org.

Debora Kuan "The Night After You Lose Your Job." Originally published in *Poetry* (July/ Aug. 2021). © 2021 by Debora Kuan. Reprinted with the permission of the author.

Patricia Smith, "When the Burning Begins" from *Treehouse of the Almighty*. Copyright © 2006 by Patricia Smith. Reprinted with the permission of Coffeehouse Press.

Jane Kenyon, "Let Evening Come" from *Collected Poems*. Copyright © 2005 by The Estate of Jane Kenyon. Reprinted with the permission of The Permissions Company, LLC on behalf of Graywolf Press, graywolfpress.org.

Timothy Donnelly, "Epitaph by His Own Hand" from *The Cloud Corporation*. Copyright 2010. Reprinted with permission of the author and Wave Books.

Carol Moldaw, "Arthritis" from *Go Figure*. Originally published in Poem-a-Day March 14, 2018. Copyright © 2018, 2024 by Carol Moldaw. Reprinted with the permission of The Permissions Company, LLC on behalf of Four Way Books, fourwaybooks.com.

Index of Poets

Tyler Mills is a poet, essayist, and educator. She is the author of *City Scattered* (Snowbound Chapbook Award, Tupelo Press, 2022); *Hawk Parable* (Akron Poetry Prize, University of Akron Press, 2019); *Tongue Lyre* (Crab Orchard Series in Poetry First Book Award, Southern Illinois University Press, 2013); and co-author with Kendra DeColo of *Low Budget Movie* (Diode Editions Chapbook Prize, Diode Editions, 2021). Her memoir, *The Bomb Cloud* (Unbound Edition Press, March, 2024), received a Literature Grant from the Café Royal Foundation NYC. Her poems have appeared in *The New Yorker*, *The Guardian*, *The New Republic*, *The Believer*, and *Poetry*, and her essays in *AGNI*, *Brevity*, *Copper Nickel*, *River Teeth*, and *The Rumpus*. The recipient of residencies from Yaddo, Ragdale, the Bethany Arts Community, and the Vermont Studio Center, as well as fellowships from Bread Loaf, Sewanee, and the Kenyon Review Writers Workshop, Tyler Mills teaches for Sarah Lawrence College's Writing Institute and the Provincetown Fine Arts Work Center's 24PearlStreet. She lives in Brooklyn, NY and can be found at www.tylermills.com.